THE LIGHT OF KNOWLEDGE

THE LIGHT OF KNOWLEDGE

How James Bradley and the Lane Rebels
Forever Changed American Higher Education

JEFF AUPPERLE

WIPF & STOCK · Eugene, Oregon

THE LIGHT OF KNOWLEDGE
How James Bradley and the Lane Rebels Forever Changed
American Higher Education

Copyright © 2021 Jeff Aupperle. All rights reserved. Except for brief quotations in critical publications or reviews, no part of this book may be reproduced in any manner without prior written permission from the publisher. Write: Permissions, Wipf and Stock Publishers, 199 W. 8th Ave., Suite 3, Eugene, OR 97401.

Wipf & Stock
An Imprint of Wipf and Stock Publishers
199 W. 8th Ave., Suite 3
Eugene, OR 97401

www.wipfandstock.com

PAPERBACK ISBN: 978-1-6667-3059-3
HARDCOVER ISBN: 978-1-6667-2230-7
EBOOK ISBN: 978-1-6667-2231-4

SEPTEMBER 17, 2021

Scriptures taken from the Holy Bible, New International Version®, NIV®. Copyright © 1973, 1978, 1984, 2011 by Biblica, Inc.™ Used by permission of Zondervan. All rights reserved worldwide. www.zondervan.com The "NIV" and "New International Version" are trademarks registered in the United States Patent and Trademark Office by Biblica, Inc.™

Contents

Foreword | ix

Introduction | xi

Chapter 1
Oberlin: The Great Pioneer | 1
    A Time for Protest | 1
    Cultured Ornaments of Society | 4
    Antebellum Higher Education, 1790–1861 | 7
    Student Protest | 13
    Civil Rights Era | 14
    Contemporary Student Protest | 16
    Summary | 18

Chapter 2
James Bradley and the Lane Rebels | 19
    James Bradley Arrives at Lane | 28
    The History of Lane Theological Seminary | 29
    The Slavery Question | 33
    Prelude to the Debates | 38

Chapter 3
The Debates at Lane Theological Seminary | 41
 The Perfect Storm | 41
 The Testimony of James Bradley | 46
 Structure and Content | 49
 Immediate Aftermath | 53

Chapter 4
Trustees Upon the Stage | 56
 Peculiar Academic Phenomenon | 56
 Report of the Trustees | 58
 Acquiesced in Arbitrary Rule | 64

Chapter 5
The Statement of Reasons | 71
 A Spirit of Free Inquiry | 71
 An Inalienable Right | 75
 The Exigencies of the Age | 77
 Unchecked Power | 82
 James Bradley | 88
 Critical Reception | 92

Chapter 6
Rebels with a Cause | 94
 A Seminary of Our Own | 95
 Oberlin | 98
 Shipherd's Plea | 103

CHAPTER 7
CASTE HAS FOUND NO ASYLUM | 109
  Rising Tensions | 109
  A Revolutionary Policy | 112
  James Bradley at Oberlin | 118

EPILOGUE
THE LIGHT OF KNOWLEDGE | 122
  Lane Theological Seminary | 123
  Oberlin College | 125
  Student Protest and Higher Education | 128
  Recommendations for Practice | 128
  Conclusion | 129

Bibliography | 133

Foreword

ON A COLD NOVEMBER morning in Philadelphia, I chose to make the one-mile walk from my hotel to the Presbyterian Historical Society. Having arrived at the Society, I opened up a folder to find what I had come to see—the original document that was signed by James Bradley, along with his fellow Lane Theological Seminary Rebels, to signify their decision to leave the seminary in 1834. Even as I held that original document in my hands in Philadelphia, my kids were being dropped off at school for the day and the Calling and Career Office that I direct at Taylor University was opening its doors to the students. The truth is, books are not possible without the sacrifice of many, and I am so grateful to many who gave of themselves so that I could pursue this academic journey.

To my wife Rachel, the strongest woman I know, I love you and am thankful for your steady presence and encouragement. To Reid, Jaelynn, and Jonas, I love you. Thank you for cheering me on! I sincerely hope that when the opportunity comes you will act with the same conviction as the so-called Rebels you'll read about in the pages to come. Thanks to my dad, who has always been in my corner even when so much was uncertain when we made the decision to pursue this calling to the work of higher education—Dad, I share this accomplishment with you and Mom. I am also so grateful to my dissertation chair, Dr. Kandace Hinton, for her support and guidance throughout my doctoral studies. To the many family and friends—too many to count—who have encouraged me, prayed for me, and inspired me, thank you.

Foreword

Finally, to my students, the reason I do what I do, the students you will read about in this study blazed a trail worth following. I pray that your education will also be filled with the light of knowledge as you seek to create a world where it is easier to love.

Introduction

WHY OBERLIN? THE STORY of this book began with that question as I sat in a class about the history of American higher education. Much of the history of higher education in this country finds its roots somewhere along the East Coast. The story of Oberlin defies that trend, but then again, as you'll soon find out, that was Oberlin's way. In a time where the educational opportunities afforded women and students of color were limited at best, Oberlin flung their doors open wide, admitting students regardless of race or gender. Fanny Jackson Cooper, a Black woman, was a member of the teaching faculty at Oberlin in 1864—one hundred years before the Civil Rights Act was written into law.

So again, why Oberlin? The pursuit of an answer to this question led me to the Oberlin Archives, where I first read about the Lane Rebels of 1835. After an additional trip to Oberlin's archives, I set my course for Pennsylvania to view the original documents of the Lane Theological Seminary at the Presbyterian Historical Society in downtown Philadelphia. It was there in Philadelphia, nearly five hundred miles from Oberlin, that I saw the handwriting of James Bradley, the emancipated slave that defied death, purchased his own freedom, and became the first Black student by way of official policy at the Oberlin Collegiate Institute in 1835.

The answer to my question was becoming increasingly clear: conviction. Bradley's conviction that higher education, the light of knowledge, as he described it, was worth sacrificing everything for. The Lane Rebels' conviction that slavery was America's most

Introduction

pressing sin and that it must be eradicated immediately. The Oberlin community's conviction that God's kingdom was not divided by gender or race, so why would any seek to separate in such a manner while here on earth?

I sat in this class during the summer of 2016. The deaths of Alton Sterling and Philando Castile separated by two days in July of 2016 had raised some important questions that I felt duty-bound to address. I have found the heroic story of James Bradley to be a compelling reason to answer them and to do so in community with family, friends, and a society so deeply divided on matters of race. In a time where many are searching for ways to respond to their internal conviction for racial justice in the United States, it is good to be reminded of the stories of those who came before us and put their lives on the line to see dreams of justice come to fruition.

Historical studies within the realm of educational research present a distinctive opportunity for each new generation of researchers to reinterpret past events in order to develop understanding of the present. The study of historical actions within the realm of higher education holds potential to bring clarity to present events and, in turn, inform a "sense of common purpose about education in US society."[1]

John Thelin posed an important question at the end of his foundational volume on the history of American higher education. Responding to the oft-cited criticism that higher education has drifted from its educational purposes, Thelin asked, "How might this be set aright?"[2] Thelin offered an answer that is an appropriate one for the overarching purposes of inquiry and for this particular study of history, contending that the good work of historical research will be most pertinent if its readers apply the lessons of the past toward interpreting the present and the creation of a better future. Thelin posited that history holds great power when it "informs a new generation of higher education readers and leaders

---

1. McMillan and Schumacher, *Research in Education*, 427.
2. Thelin, *History of Higher Education*, 398.

INTRODUCTION

of the insights that make all stakeholders thoughtfully concerned about connecting past and present to assure a sound future."³

The design of this study, then, was intended to provide a robust response to the question: Why Oberlin? And, while doing so, ask the question: Why not here? To do so, I dove deeply into the historical actions of James Bradley and the Lane Theological Seminary Rebels as a means of informing a new generation of higher education readers and leaders toward a thoughtful connection of past and present toward the assurance of a sound future. In light of the historic levels of student protest in contemporary higher education, the ambition of this study was that contemporary university students—my students—might connect the actions of their predecessors to modern forms of protest, infused with dialogue, toward the assurance of a sound future.

3. Thelin, *History of Higher Education*, 398.

Chapter 1

OBERLIN: THE GREAT PIONEER

A TIME FOR PROTEST

ON A BLEAK WINTER day in December 2015, as winter break approached the campus of Oberlin College, a group of distraught students composed a letter of protest addressed to the office of the President, Dr. Marvin Krislov. Embedded in the opening paragraph of their impassioned appeal was a strong accusation, "Oberlin College unapologetically acts as an unethical institution, antithetical to its historical mission."[1] The substance of the petition, addressed to Krislov, the Board of Trustees, and other members of academic leadership, detailed multiple grievances, all of which stemmed from what the students deemed to be clear and convincing acts of racial discrimination throughout their student experience at Oberlin College. The letter methodically delineated a series of demands in response to these perceived wrongs, ranging from the immediate dismissal of some faculty members while granting immediate tenure to others, substantial curricular changes, and a revision of grading methods.

Such a letter had become increasingly part of the university experience in America. The letter from the students at Oberlin

---

1. Oberlin, "Student Letter of Protest," para. 1.

The Light of Knowledge

College came at a time of ubiquitous student protest in higher education. In this phenomenon that transpired on campuses across the country, "student protesters made demands to right what they see as historic wrongs—demands for greater faculty diversity, new courses, public apologies, administrators' ousting" at more than fifty institutions.[2] Three central issues created the conditions for the surge in protest; namely, an unprecedented increase in sexual assault on campus, rising tuition along with the subsequent issue of increasing student debt, and, most prominently, rising tensions related to a steady increase in campus incidences of racial discrimination and injustice. In providing context to the Oberlin College students' angst, Krislov acknowledged the moment, noting that the letter of protest arrived at his office "against a backdrop of events at colleges and universities across the country, including Oberlin College, prompting passionate discussions and demonstrations related to the existence of racism in American higher education."[3]

What made this particular letter stand out, however, was its place of origin. Oberlin College, a small liberal arts institution in Lorain County, Ohio, has a storied history marked by an enduring commitment to providing equality in educational opportunity to all students irrespective of their race or gender. In fact, Krislov cited this rich heritage when responding to the students' letter publicly, noting that Oberlin College has historically been sustained through a "consensus-driven process that includes dialogue in which dissenting voices are heard."[4]

In this particular case, President Krislov determined that not every voice had been heard. On account of their rich institutional history, full of examples of civil dialogue, Krislov detailed his decision not to take immediate action on the students' demands due to the many ways in which the letter of protest "explicitly rejects the notion of collaborative engagement."[5] Prominent in Krislov's decision was his diagnosis of the absence of dialogue, a key component

2. Dickey, "Revolution," 1.
3. Krislov, "Response," 1.
4. Krislov, "Response," 1.
5. Krislov, "Response," 1.

that had been consistently present within the forms of protest that had, from his perspective, engendered positive change at the institution over the course of its 183 years of delivering higher education in Lorain County, Ohio, up until that point in time.

Foremost among these many demonstrations of protest were the actions of some of Oberlin College's first students—also known as the Lane Rebels—a protest inspiring landmark change at Oberlin, but which actually traces its roots to nineteenth-century Cincinnati. Concurrent with debates transpiring at many college campuses in the antebellum North, students at the Lane Theological Seminary congregated to openly examine the contentious question of slavery in America in 1834. Over the course of eighteen February nights, student abolitionists and their counterparts, students representing the position of the American Colonization Society, argued their case. Halfway through those spirited meetings, a young seminarian, an emancipated slave by the name of James Bradley, stood before the gathered students and faculty and "withered and scorched the pro-slavery arguments."[6]

Moved by compelling arguments and impassioned testimony, the students at Lane Theological Seminary resolved toward revolutionary action for the cause of abolition. The so-called "Rebels" formed an anti-slavery society and went to work in bringing this issue to light throughout the surrounding neighborhoods in Cincinnati. And, when the Lane Theological Seminary Board of Trustees moved to silence their efforts, the deep-seated conviction of these students ultimately led to a mass exodus from the seminary. Most of these exiles would later find a collegiate home at Oberlin. The decision to attend Oberlin College, however, hinged upon a series of prescient conditions. Primary among these conditions was the establishment, as a matter of official policy, of what would become the first institutional course of action for the admission of Black students anywhere in American higher education. These two referenced incidences of student protest at Oberlin College, separated by two centuries, are emblematic of the potent, though sometimes enigmatic, nature of student protest to provoke

6. Fletcher, *History of Oberlin*, 153.

significant change. They also serve as salient examples of the critical role dialogue can play within protest in determining its efficacy. Concerning dialogue, Paulo Freire posited, "The correct method for a revolutionary leadership to employ in the task of liberation is, therefore, not 'libertarian propaganda.' Nor can the leadership merely 'implant' in the oppressed a belief in freedom... The correct method lies in dialogue."[7] The power of dialogue, inspiring both reflection and action, holds potential for channeling student protest toward lasting change, both in higher education and society at large.

Extensive barriers have stood in the path of Black students pursuing higher education in American history. Yet, within that history, there are important stories to be told—a collective of stories of pioneers who overcame substantial obstacles along the path toward the realization of this noble end. Among the few that endured the arduous path is the story of an emancipated slave by the name of James L. Bradley. Bradley, along with his fellow exiles from Lane Theological Seminary, would embrace the principles of dialogue, reflection, and action to inspire revolutionary change, both at Oberlin College and, subsequently, all of American higher education. The ripple effect of their actions for Black students' pursuit of higher education at Oberlin College was profound. "Where did Black men finish college? Oberlin College, an abolitionist institution in Ohio, perhaps trained two-thirds of them... it was the great pioneer in the work of blotting out the color-line in colleges."[8]

CULTURED ORNAMENTS OF SOCIETY

American higher education has seemingly always had a bit of an existential crisis. The rite of passage marked by learning and development that so richly transpires on college campuses is often juxtaposed with the economic and utilitarian ends of a college degree. This contrast often leads to well-worn arguments surrounding

---

7. Freire, *Pedagogy of the Oppressed*, 67.
8. Gavins, "Historical Overview," 17.

Oberlin: The Great Pioneer

questions about both the true purpose and the value proposition of higher education. It has been this way from the very beginning.

The colonial period of higher education in America began in Cambridge, Massachusetts, with the establishment of Harvard in 1636. Higher education was deemed an essential institution for the creation of a new culture in colonial America. Higher education historian Frederick Rudolph described Harvard's necessity: "Unable to set the world straight as Englishmen in England, the Puritan settlers of Massachusetts intended to set it straight as Englishmen in the New World."[9] Harvard was inaugurated with a divinely inspired charter—biblical training and the pious development of the young men in the new land. "The College would train the schoolmasters, the divines, the rulers, the cultured ornaments of society—the men who would spell the difference between civilization and barbarism."[10]

Harvard was thought to be essential to sustain the dream of the first settlers. The necessity of Harvard is further substantiated by the establishment of multiple institutions of higher learning with similar missions in keeping up with the expansion of American population during the colonial period. As this brave new world was taking shape along the shores of the Atlantic, "it needed leaders disciplined by knowledge and learning; it needed followers disciplined by leaders; it needed order."[11]

From its inception, Harvard, like many societal institutions of the colonial period, was buoyed by the economic benefits of slavery. American historian, Craig Steven Wilder noted that at the time of Harvard's two hundredth anniversary, it "was also nearing the bicentennial of its intimate engagement with Atlantic slavery."[12] In the minds of their founders, the perceived need of leadership development justified the establishment of five colleges—Harvard,

---

9. Rudolph, *American College*, 5.
10. Rudolph, *American College*, 6.
11. Rudolph, *American College*, 7.
12. Wilder, *Ebony and Ivy*, 2.

William and Mary, Yale, Codrington, and New Jersey—that were all "major beneficiaries of the African slave trade and slavery."[13]

By the time of the Revolutionary War, there were nine colleges serving the growing American colonies. "This planting of temples of piety and intellect in the wilderness was no accident. Nor was it stubbornness, foolhardiness, even the booster spirit of pioneering people which placed at the disposal of American youth so extraordinary a number."[14] The steady increase of institutions of higher education in the colonial period is emblematic of the conviction of the country's founders. From their perspective, they simply "could not afford to leave its shaping to whim, fate, accident, indecision, or carelessness."[15] Sustaining nine institutions in the colonial period was possible, in part, due to an economy that flourished from the slave trade.

At the conclusion of the Revolutionary War, the establishment of a new country, regulated by a newly minted Constitution, created the conditions for democratic debate of all forms about what should henceforth define the American experience. The colleges and universities that were established in the colonial period provided the architectural ambiance for the ongoing conversations about the most pressing questions facing the formation of a just society. Thus, college campuses became one of the primary stages upon which the debate on the morality of the slave trade and slavery in America intensified.

A popular idea among higher education leadership at the time, most prominently held by Yale president Jeremiah Day, was the strategy of colonization. Colonizationists sought to enable the migration of free African Americans back to Africa, instead of seeking their full emancipation rights in the United States. "New England's colonizationists cast African Americans as a threat to democracy and social order . . . they silenced debate about slavery and vehemently attacked abolitionism."[16] As American higher

13. Wilder, *Ebony and Ivy*, 17.
14. Rudolph, *American College*, 3.
15. Rudolph, *American College*, 6.
16. Wilder, *Ebony and Ivy*, 2.

education entered into the antebellum era of American history, the discussion on slavery would not be silenced. Rather, it was only magnified in the classrooms and across the campuses of the early nation's colleges and universities.

ANTEBELLUM HIGHER EDUCATION, 1790-1861

The antebellum period, 1790–1861, was a time of considerable expansion for higher education in America. John Thelin described the period as one of "extreme innovation and consumerism, with virtually no government accountability or regulation."[17] The rapid development of the enterprise of higher education during this period was not one of timidity or even what some may describe as basic common sense; rather, it was an era of growth that displayed what was perhaps a naive, but certainly undaunted, faith in America's future. The burgeoning landscape of higher education in that era was built with a firm belief in the "unquestionable capacity of Americans to achieve a better world. In the founding of colleges, reason could not combat the romantic belief in endless progress."[18]

As such, the antebellum era saw the establishment of an eclectic assortment of educational institutions with unique organizational missions. As the population grew and a new culture rapidly developed throughout the country, new institutions were regularly formed to meet the educational and economic needs to sustain both the expanding cities and territories and the expanding beliefs and denominations within them. In addition to educational and economic ends, religious zeal led to the proliferation of small faith-based institutions of higher education designed in alignment with specific denominational allegiance. It was denominationalism, above anything else, that was the primary factor for expansion during the antebellum period, specifically in the founding of "eleven colleges in Kentucky before 1865, twenty-one in Illinois

---

17. Thelin, *History of Higher Education*, 41.
18. Rudolph, *American College*, 48–49.

before 1868, [and] thirteen in Iowa before 1869 . . . By 1861 denominational ambition had covered the country with colleges."[19]

As the enterprise of higher education multiplied, it also played host to the debate of some of the most contentious questions associated with the formation of an innovative and entrepreneurial society. Among those questions, perhaps no other was debated as much or with the same intensity during the antebellum era as the question on the morality of slavery in America. Widespread debates transpired in formal and informal settings during the antebellum period, including heated exchanges between colonization societies and their rival abolitionist counterparts. Consequently, the rising climate surrounding the issue of slavery and the debate of its merits on college campuses was a constant point of concern for many faculty members, presidents, and most assuredly the board of trustees members in fulfilling what they deemed to be their primary academic mission.

Within this antebellum period in American history, the year of 1834 would prove to be significant in response to the question of slavery. Twenty-seven years yet removed from the beginning of the Civil War in the United States, the undercurrent toward the eradication of the practice of slavery was gaining momentum. Across the Atlantic, the enduring work of William Wilberforce and the Clapham Sect had come to fruition; what may have been seen as an outright impossibility at the inception of their efforts came to pass in the summer of 1834 when the Slavery Abolition Act of 1833 became the law of the land in the United Kingdom.

Across the ocean, a fledgling country, just over fifty years from the liberation of a revolutionary war, proved to be not yet ready for such a declaration. While there may have been many who morally objected to the practice of slavery, tangled webs of selfish pride, assumed prestige, and ostensible economic benefits perpetuated a vicious cycle. Those who dissented had to practice caution in discerning when and where such views were safe to espouse; 1834 also marked the year of vicious riots in New York City targeted at those who were sympathetic to the abolitionist cause.

19. Rudolph, *American College*, 55.

Oberlin: The Great Pioneer

The issue of slavery was pervasive in the 1834 version of the United States, seemingly touching every area of American life regardless of industry or geography. Higher education in America was by no means isolated from the matter. "The academy never stood apart from American slavery—in fact, it stood beside church and state as the third pillar of a civilization built on bondage."[20] Higher education, then, in some critical ways, was an ideal crucible for the question of slavery as developing minds began to challenge assumptions and dared to explore an alternative American reality.

Wilder identified the Reverend Ralph Randolph Gurley, Yale class of 1818 and the principal agent of the American Colonization Society, as a key player who "chose colleges as a battlefield in the war to defeat 'our enemies—the abolitionists.'"[21] As the American Colonization Society targeted campuses across the country, antislavery societies were often formed to rise and meet the challenge of their counterparts leading to long-lasting and many times contentious debates that mark the histories of many American institutions. Institutions such as Western Reserve College in Ohio, Oneida Institute in New York, Lane Theological Seminary in Cincinnati, Hanover College in Indiana, and Amherst College in Massachusetts are salient historical examples of college campuses where this specific debate intensified during the antebellum era, leaving a substantial ripple effect on the students and communities that comprised these campuses for generations.

A historical review of higher education in the antebellum period reveals that there were similar events transpiring concurrently with the specific events highlighted in this book at Lane Theological Seminary and Oberlin College. One such example can be found in the archives at Amherst College. The university leadership had determined they had heard enough of the students' so-called discussions and took action to silence all discussions of slavery in 1834, the same year that parallel action was taken at Lane Theological Seminary. In similar fashion to the events at Lane, the Amherst students, buoyed by theological conviction on

---

20. Wilder, *Ebony and Ivy*, 11.
21. Wilder, *Ebony and Ivy*, 266.

the sinfulness of slavery, rebuffed their academic leaders' attempts to silence their fervor. The student response was originally published in the *New York Evangelist* in 1835:

> We look again over two millions of our countrymen—we hear the clanking of their chains—we listen to their moving pleas for deliverance—their deep-toned wailings are borne to us on every breeze... We would gladly comply with your requests, if we could do it consistently with the dictates of conscience, and the wants and woes of perishing millions.[22]

In 1834-35, multiple events with remarkable similarity transpired across the landscape of American higher education. These events effectively mark the time and, in doing so, place the events at Lane Theological Seminary and Oberlin College in their proper historical context. In 1834, the American Colonization Society held annual meetings where Yale president Jeremiah Day served as Vice President. "The great majority of the crusade's adherents had serious doubts about the spiritual capacity of and social potential of Black peoples, African or American."[23] And yet, even in the face of seemingly insurmountable odds, Black students in the antebellum era continued along the arduous path in pursuit of higher education.

Education was essentially prohibited for slaves in antebellum America and largely ignored by Black freedmen. Yet, in defiance to the status quo, there were courageous Black students that persisted and sought liberation via the transformational power of education. The culture of intellectual supremacy espoused by leaders like Jeremiah Day and the American Colonization Society was felt more broadly across the landscape of antebellum higher education in America. All of this created the conditions for hardship and substantial barriers for Black students who pursued higher learning.

In a historical review of American higher education during the antebellum period, there were a total of twenty-eight Black college graduates by 1860. However, during this restrictive time

22. Wilder, *Ebony and Ivy*, 269.
23. Wilder, *Ebony and Ivy*, 272.

in the history of higher education, Oberlin College developed into a beacon of hope for the education of African American students. The very first of these hopeful students was James Bradley. Bradley, after working tirelessly to purchase his freedom in the slaveholding South, journeyed north and was able to begin his studies at Lane Theological Seminary in Cincinnati. Bradley would later join the other Lane Theological Seminary Rebels at Oberlin Collegiate Institute.

Historians of higher education have consistently identified Oberlin College for its groundbreaking policies in advancing the cause of equality for all students regardless of race or gender. Oberlin College has enabled a multitude of students to pursue the opportunities presented by higher education in America. Following the conclusive vote by the Board of Trustees in 1835, the ensuing establishment of Asa Mahan as President along with the additions of influential instructors like Charles Finney, John Morgan, and others created a magnetic environment that drew African American students toward this blossoming campus in northern Ohio.

The conviction and courage of the so-called Lane Rebels, this group of advanced and thoughtful students at Lane Theological Seminary, paved the way to open the floodgates for educational opportunity for African American students at Oberlin Collegiate Institute in the antebellum era. The founding of Oberlin College in 1833 is a major landmark in the story of access and progress for African American students in the history of American higher education. In addition to its founding and the establishment of the first admissions policy without regard to race in 1835, the graduation of the first Black student at Oberlin College, George B. Vashon in 1844, is noteworthy. Vashon would later implement his learnings at Oberlin College to contribute to the founding of Howard University in Washington, DC, in 1867.

Oberlin educated Black students with distinction during a time that most colleges and universities in American higher education were sustained through extensive connections to the Transatlantic Slave Trade. Wilder argues that "American colleges were not innocent or passive beneficiaries of conquest and colonial slavery."[24] In similar fashion to their church and state brethren within the young country, universities readily benefited from the perpetuation of slavery. University leadership were all too often active participants in the viscious cycle of growing and establishing a burgeoning society on the backs of slaves.

Over the course of time, landmark events in the history of higher education would gradually open the door substantially wider for African American students. The groundbreaking policy at Oberlin College to admit students without respect to race in 1835—to be described in detail throughout this book—would be pivotal in regard to setting into motion a trajectory of increased opportunity for African American students. Along the upward trajectory, the Morrill Act of 1862, the decision rendered in Brown v. Board of Education in 1954, and the establishment of the Civil Rights Act in 1964 are decisive moments in slowly changing the narrative of African American students' access to higher education.

The antebellum period in American higher education—the historical context from which this story is told—is marked by the extensive expansion of colleges and universities in keeping with the rapid growth of the country. The swift establishment and development of these institutions of higher education, however, are not simply stories of remarkable progress rooted in faith in the American dream. For many inhabitants of a developing American society, the pursuit of higher education was seen as only something possible for the privileged few. While some institutions sought to provide increased access to all regardless of gender or race, the academy in antebellum America often served to reinforce the established order of race and gender and held hostage the associated rights and privileges of the educational opportunity that they offered.

> In the decades before the Civil War, American scholars claimed a new public role as the racial guardians of the United States . . . The intellectual roots of the cyclical political and social assaults upon Native Americans,

24. Wilder, *Ebony and Ivy*, 11.

Oberlin: The Great Pioneer

African Americans, Jews, Irish, and Asians can be traced back to this scholarly obsession with race.[25]

STUDENT PROTEST

In addition to these issues of inequality and access, another narrative entrenched in the complex history of higher education in America is the constant of student protest. Demonstrations of student protest can be traced back to medieval universities and are common to the histories of institutions of higher education wherever they are found. From the renowned Great Butter Rebellion at Harvard in 1766 to the devastating Vietnam War protest on the campus of Kent State University nearly two hundred years later, the historical account of American higher education has been marked by student protest across the generations. In particular, the student movements of the 1960s and 1970s have left an indelible mark on the formation of a more just society both within the confines of the campuses where they transpired and American society at-large.

Student protest has existed as long as colleges themselves. The chosen forms and methods for such protests, however, have varied greatly. While student protest has been a powerful channel to prompt understanding and provoke change, it has also been a means for destructive ends and, at times, been assessed to have done more damage than good at the institutions in which they have transpired. Thus, one of the aspirations in doing this historical research was to gain understanding toward the constructive nature of dialogue within protest. If the long-term effectiveness of protest is determined, in part, by the measure of dialogue present, what can be learned from historical research that might serve to both inform the present and promote a hopeful future?

In considering those historical moments, specifically the student movements of the 1960s, M. K. Jennings integrated the generational thesis in researching the lives of students involved

---

25. Wilder, *Ebony and Ivy*, 273.

in those salient protest demonstrations in American history.[26] The central tenet of the generational thesis is that participation in activities during the formative years of life can serve to predict participation over the course of a lifetime. Over thirty-two years, Jennings tracked the political activity of the graduating class of 1969 and discovered that the students who actively participated in protests, during a time of great dissent in American history, were more likely to remain active in the political process throughout their lives than the students who did not. The conclusions of Jennings' research indicated the enduring impact of participation in student protest over the course of a lifetime.

However, the resultant impact of student protest is not only discovered in the individual lives of those who protested but on the campuses where they happened. Similar to what has transpired on the small campus at Oberlin College, historical occurrences of student protest often create the conditions for an activist subculture, increasing the likelihood of further demonstrations in a campus environment. The nature of student protest is one that has lasting effects both in the students' lives and the different campuses where they transpire. In studying hotbeds of activism, Van Dyke's 1998 study revealed the ways in which the student and civil rights movements of the 1960s positively influenced one another.

CIVIL RIGHTS ERA

In the face of vast inequities, African American students have often chosen the communication channel of student protest in order to shed light on injustice. Choosing activism as a response to racial segregation, inequality, and injustice, the lasting impact of their actions is still felt today on the campuses, in the communities, and in the country where they transpired. Such demonstrations of protest have taken many forms over the years, from meeting to debate the question of slavery over eighteen nights in Cincinnati in 1834, to choosing to sit down at a known segregated lunch counter at

26. Jennings, "Residues of a Movement."

an F. W. Woolworth in Greensboro in 1960, to presenting a set of grievances and demands to the university president in a public demonstration on the streets of Columbia, Missouri in 2015.

In 1972, A. M. Orum conducted a study on the origins of the Black student movement of the 1960s.[27] The volume began by discussing the evening of January 31, 1960, when four North Carolina Agricultural and Technical College students' dialogue gave way to reflection, and reflection gave way to action. The following day, these four students, David Richmond, Franklin McCain, Joseph McNeil, and Ezell Blair Jr., sat down at a segregated lunch counter at the F. W. Woolworth in Greensboro, North Carolina, and, in direct disregard for the law of land, asked for four cups of coffee.

In seeking to understand the underlying motivations of the students who participated in the Black student movement, Orum analyzed the responses of a national sample of college graduates from the spring of 1964. Orum presented a hypothesis of three independent sets of conditions that influenced student engagement in protest activity: personal background and values; experiences and attitudes related to college life; and variations of college settings. However, Orum concluded that, interestingly, personal background and values played little role in the students' motivation to join the Black student protests of the early 1960s.

Instead, beyond any personal interest or circumstance, student engagement in the Black student movement was motivated by the social and economic condition of the people in their neighborhood. According to Orum, students were driven less by some form of perceived intrinsic benefit and more by a communal sense of belonging and accountability to the welfare of the people who embodied their community. Orum contended at the time that the true impact of the Black student activism may not be fully understood for many years. Orum's conclusion is instructive toward further reinforcing the idea that demonstrations of student protest cannot be measured by merely the impact of a moment, but of a movement—the larger narrative that unfolds for many years to come as one generation passes on the torch to the next.

27. Orum, *Black Students in Protest.*

THE LIGHT OF KNOWLEDGE

A similar story from the civil rights era can be found at Rutgers University in New Jersey. The Black student protest at Rutgers in the late 1960s comprises, in effect, a case study in student protest for racial equality. In the 1968–69 academic year at Rutgers, student dialogue and reflection led to action to bring injustice to light. Pained by the underrepresentation of Black students and leaders in comparison to what they observed in their surrounding community, students presented a list of grievances and demands to the Rutgers University Board of Directors. Institutional leadership would later respond with an initiative specifically focused on providing unprecedented opportunity to educationally and economically disadvantaged students in the communities and neighborhoods near the Rutgers campus.

This case study at Rutgers aptly exhibits the potential long-term impact of thoughtful student protest to inspire revolutionary action that can come by way of educational access and opportunity. In similar fashion, the research presented in Rael's 2001 volume on Black identity and Black protest in the antebellum North further indicated the revolutionary nature of protest toward the establishment of a more just society.[28] Rael described the historical intricacies of Black identity development and protest activity—arguing that the very foundations of Black identity during the antebellum period were forged through an appeal to the hearts and minds of those who held power.

CONTEMPORARY STUDENT PROTEST

This chapter began by referencing the protest of the Oberlin students in 2016. Their letter of protest is representative of contemporary student protest that still serves as a compelling channel for students to bring about awareness and, sometimes, lasting changes on their respective campuses within American higher education. Oberlin College has a rich history of being an educational environment that encourages students to raise questions, challenge

---

28. Rael, *Black Identity*.

Oberlin: The Great Pioneer

tyranny, and seek meaningful change. Likewise, the nation's oldest institution of higher education, Harvard, has a long lineage of protest on its hallowed Cambridge grounds. Harvard has played host to student protest from the colonial period, to the renowned student rebellion of 1969, to the protest of students in 2018 in response to the forcible arrest of a Black student, which inspired a group of students to organize to bring light to injustice.

In addition, contemporary events at the University of Missouri offer another noteworthy example of the change that protest can produce. The university, located in Columbia, Missouri, is about one hundred miles away from the smaller town of Ferguson where, in August of 2014, an unarmed Black teenager named Michael Brown was shot and killed. The demonstrations of student activism at the University of Missouri traced their roots back to that tragic event. In reporting on the protests for *The Chronicle of Higher Education* Stripling posited, "For students, the incident brought to the fore longstanding concerns about racism on the campus, which they described as hostile to minorities."[29] The incident in Ferguson and ensuing unrest that drew the attention of a nation pointed to a pivotal moment for action on the campus of the University of Missouri, which ultimately resulted in the resignation of the president of the University of Missouri System among other significant changes.

In February 2016, the Higher Education Research Institute of UCLA (HERI) released findings from the 2015 national CIRP freshman survey, a survey from which data has been collected annually from freshman students across the country for over fifty years.[30] Among the freshmen surveyed in the 2015 survey, 8.5 percent responded that they have a very good chance of participating in student protests. According to HERI, that number represented the highest mark in the survey's history.

African American students scored substantially higher on that item, as 16 percent of incoming African American students reported that there was a very good chance they would participate

---

29. Stripling, *National Debate*, p. 1.
30. HERI, "The American Freshman."

in protest activity. In wring for *Time Magazine*, Dickey captured the spirit of this moment in higher education well when he wrote these words: "It's been a half century since we've seen US Colleges so roiled," noting that the survey numbers from HERI are even higher than the "eras of the military draft, the Kent State shootings, the anti-apartheid movement, and the protests against the war in Iraq."[31]

SUMMARY

From the establishment of Harvard in 1636 to the telling survey responses of college freshmen three hundred and eighty years later, the campus has long been a microcosm of the complexities that comprise American society. In keeping with this idea, the constant of student protest is emblematic of the revolutionary American spirit, serving as an effective channel to bring about necessary change in the country. Tracing back to its entanglement with the slave trade from its inception to the experiences of African American students today on the campuses of Oberlin College, Missouri, and Harvard, the American university has been an essential institution for both understanding injustice and inequality and seeking true and lasting remedies.

The antebellum era in American higher education was a critical time in changing the narrative of access and inclusion for all students regardless of race or gender. Within that history, the story of James Bradley is emblematic of the story of so many African American students who have sought the hope that comes by way of higher education in America.

---

31. Dickey, "Revolution."

Chapter 2

James Bradley and the Lane Rebels

God will help those who take part with the oppressed. Yes, blessed be his holy name! He will surely do it... God preserve you, and strengthen you in this holy cause, until the walls of prejudice are broken down, the chains burst in pieces, and men of every color meet at the feet of Jesus, speaking kind words, and looking upon each other in love, willing to live together on earth, as they hope to live in heaven!

—James Bradley, 1835[1]

THE EXPANSION OF HIGHER education in the colonial and antebellum periods of American history, from the very beginning, is inextricably linked to the economic welfare of the country. As a result, the story of higher education's rapid growth is incomplete without recognition of the many ways it economically prospered from the Atlantic slave trade. Wilder made the argument that African slavery and the Atlantic slave trade actually served to subsidize both the college and the colony. The aforementioned year of Harvard's

---

1. Bradley, "Brief Account," 690.

founding, 1636, also marked the year of the construction of a small ship named *Desire*, which would become the first slave-carrying vessel to depart from the American mainland. *Desire* would be the first of countless ships that would bring enslaved men, women, and children from Africa.

Close to a century removed from *Desire's* maiden voyage in 1636, another ship, *Catherine*, would sail across the Atlantic to the coast of Angola. The Angola coast would become the single most important trading center in West Africa by the latter part of the eighteenth century. In sum, more than two and a half million people were taken from their homeland in Africa from the shores of the Angola coast. Two and a half million human lives, human stories, packed into overcrowded and understaffed vessels, bound for a life of slavery. The inhumane conditions of cross-Atlantic slave ships has been detailed and documented in the years since.

> Lengthy imprisonments in narrow, cramped, and filthy holds accelerated the spread of diseases during return voyages that lasted several weeks. The poor diet provided the captives delivered few nutrients. A year before *Catherine's* first voyage, a ship's surgeon had complained that mashed beans or peas mixed with salted, rotting fish and fed, sometimes forcibly, to the Africans on his ships further undermined their health.[2]

Approximately a hundred years later, another century removed from *Catherine's* first voyage and now two centuries removed from the maiden voyage of *Desire* in 1636, an emancipated slave by the name of James Bradley arrived on the campus of Lane Theological Seminary in Cincinnati, Ohio, in search of the opportunity that comes by way of higher education. Bradley first arrived in America on a slave ship after being taken from the shores of the Angola coast when he was just a toddler. Bradley's experience was not unlike so many others who "were physically and emotionally compromised by the time they were loaded into ships, having survived violent acquisition from kidnapping and raids."[3] Such was

2. Wilder, *Ebony and Ivy*, 54.
3. Wilder, *Ebony and Ivy*, 54.

James Bradley and the Lane Rebels

the case of the slavery experience of a far-too-young James Bradley. In June of 1834, Bradley wrote an autobiography that would go on to be published by Maria Lydia Child in the *Oasis*—a newspaper dedicated to publishing accurate portrayals of the realities of the slave trade. Bradley's personal story was widely reprinted.

Autobiographical accounts that convey with great detail the experiences of slaves carry ineffable power in offering an accurate portrayal of slavery's horrors. Despite their potency, few historians have chosen to pursue these important narratives. Historians have examined "all kinds of accounts written by White eyewitnesses" but have "largely rejected those written by former slaves."[4] J. W. Blassingame makes the case that the "fundamental problem confronting anyone interested in studying Black views of bondage is that the slave had few opportunities to tell what it meant to be a chattel."[5] Nonetheless, Blassingame dedicated his research and writing in order that these accounts would be available to the general public, believing that each and every story matters. In addition, the personal accounts of those who lived as slaves carry significant reliability evidenced, in part, by the fact that antebellum southern White people rarely challenged them.

Accordingly, the autobiographical work of James Bradley is critical to understanding the whole story of the Lane Theological Seminary Rebels, even that of Oberlin College. James Bradley's story is the critical hinge in the door that would ultimately fly open to scores of African American students in American higher education for generations to come. Such stories ought to be treasured: "The great slave narrative, like all great autobiography, is the work of the especially perceptive viewer and writer. In describing his personal life, the sensitive and creative writer touches a deeper reality that transcends his individuality."[6]

A thorough reading of Bradley's testimony as recorded in the *Oasis* offers insight to his experiences as a slave, the long and arduous path he journeyed toward emancipation, and the nature of

---

4. Blassingame, *Slave Testimony*, xvii.
5. Blassingame, *Slave Testimony*, xviii.
6. Osofsky, *Slave Narratives*, 10–11.

The Light of Knowledge

the motivating forces of freedom and education that carried him through his most difficult days. Bradley began his account with a cautious preface that frames the entire piece, as his every thought of days gone by carries with it the deep sorrow of his demeaned and tearful past. Yet, Bradley seemingly finds strength in his yearning for liberty and the joy he has found in its discovery. He wrote of a past marked by hope deferred and the pervasive notion that he may very well have had to accept that his life would only be defined by slavery with none to pity him.

As previously described by Wilder, the orientation of an individual to slavery often begins in a state of disorientation and pain. Bradley recalled,

> I will begin as far back as I can remember. I think I was between two and three years old when the soul-destroyers tore me from my mother's arms, somewhere in Africa, far back from the sea. They carried me a long distance to a ship; all the way, I looked back, and cried. The ship was full of men and women loaded with chains; but I was so small, they let me run about on deck.[7]

The ship that carried Bradley and countless other slaves traversed the Atlantic and completed its journey in the port of Charleston, South Carolina. Charleston was a well-known location for the arrival of slaves on America's east coast. It is estimated that in just twenty-five years from 1783 to 1808, over one hundred thousand slaves were transported through South Carolina, where they were sold throughout the thirteen colonies. There in Charleston, Bradley was purchased at a slave auction gallery and promptly taken over two hundred miles away to tiny Pendleton County, where he stayed for roughly six months. He was then sold again, this time to a Mr. Bradley where he was given the name by which he would henceforth be known. Bradley generously remembered his time with Mr. Bradley as a period where he was treated better than most; however, those memories are tarnished by moments of fear and pain. Bradley recalled specific instances

---

7. Bradley, "Brief Account," 687.

of being "tormented with kicks and knocks more than I can tell."[8] Bradley recounted a story from when he was only about nine years old where his master "struck me so hard that I fell down and lost my senses. I remained thus some time, and when I came to myself, he told me he thought he had killed me."[9]

Having been beaten nearly to the point of death at the age of nine, Bradley recounted another time where his master struck him so hard with a currycomb—a heavy tool used to groom horses—the knob of the comb sunk into his head. In describing his days as a slave under Mr. Bradley, James wrote, "I have said that I had food enough; I wish I could say as much concerning my clothing. But I let that subject alone; because I cannot think of any suitable words to use in telling you."[10]

Bradley described a life defined by relentless labor. He detailed a typical workday that began with the rising of the sun and lasted until dark with only a momentary break at noon for food. The intense and unremitting nature of the work led to him becoming severely ill for a long stretch of time. In the midst of his sickness, he was resented by his master who no longer found use for him. Bradley recalled,

> My master came to me one day, and hearing me groan with pain, he said, "This fellow will never be of any more use to me—I would as soon knock him in the head, as if he were an opossum." His children sometimes came in, and shook axes and knives at me, as if they were about to knock me on the head.[11]

Having survived multiple threats to his life, a fortuitous turn of events led to a move to the Arkansas Territory and ultimately the death of his owner. Bradley continued to work for the family, but now, as a young teenager, James had the audacity to begin

---

8. Bradley, "Brief Account," 687.
9. Bradley, "Brief Account," 687.
10. Bradley, "Brief Account," 687.
11. Bradley, "Brief Account," 687.

to dream of freedom. Slavery was all he had ever known, and he longed for liberation. Bradley described his yearning for freedom:

> My master had kept me ignorant of everything he could. I was never told anything about God, or my own soul. Yet from the time I was fourteen years old, I used to think a great deal about freedom. It was my heart's desire; I could not keep it out of my mind. Many a sleepless night I have spent in tears, because I was a slave. I looked back on all I had suffered—and when I looked ahead, all was dark and hopeless bondage. My heart ached to feel within me the life of liberty.[12]

Moved by the dream of liberty, Bradley began to work tirelessly to purchase his freedom. Regularly sleeping only three hours a night, Bradley would get up long before dawn to craft collars for horses, plaited husks by hand. Bradley could make two collars a week and sell them for fifty cents each. Bradley described his work:

> One summer, I tried to take two or three hours from my sleep every night; but found that I grew weak, and I was obliged to sleep more. With my first money I bought a pig. The next year I earned for myself about thirteen dollars; and the next about thirty. There was a good deal of wild land in the neighborhood that belonged to Congress. I used to go out with my hoe, and dig up little patches, which I planted with corn, and got up in the night to tend it. My hogs were fattened with this corn, and I used to sell a number each year. Besides this, I used to raise small patches of tobacco, and sell it to buy more corn for my pigs. In this way I worked for five years; at the end of which time, after taking out my losses, I found that I had earned one hundred and sixty dollars.[13]

Years of sleepless nights and tireless work had earned Bradley enough to invest in himself. He used his money to purchase his own time so that he could dedicate even more of his energy to this work. The sheer magnitude of work realized in what Bradley

12. Bradley, "Brief Account," 687.
13. Bradley, "Brief Account," 688.

accomplished is simply remarkable. As he labored, the current that carried him forward, the impetus for this extraordinary effort, was the daring and irrepressible hope of freedom. Bradley described this hope as one that "stung my nerves and braced up my soul so much, that I could do with very little sleep or rest. I could do a great deal more work than I was ever able to do before."[14] Over the next two years, years that were filled with diligent and efficient work, Bradley earned enough to feed and clothe himself while clearing three hundred dollars of profit. Again, James doubled down and invested in his own time again. He moved another two hundred and fifty miles west to increase his earnings. A year and a half later, in 1833, James Bradley had earned enough to buy his freedom, paying from his own pocket the price for his liberty.

Upon purchasing his freedom, Bradley immediately set course for the free state of Ohio. Bradley traveled north knowing there were schools that existed in free states that allowed Black students to attend class and pursue an education. Bradley's slave odyssey ended when he left what would later become the Confederate South by way of crossing the Ohio River into the city of Cincinnati, Ohio. Upon his arrival in Cincinnati, he learned of a local institution known as Lane Theological Seminary. Bradley had "for years been praying to God that my dark mind might see the light of knowledge."[15] Having recently gained his freedom, Bradley now focused on another long-held dream, the pursuit of education.

To James's delight the small seminary graciously granted his request and allowed him to begin to take courses at the school. Not only was he welcomed by the faculty and administration, he was welcomed by his fellow students. Bradley described the spirit of goodwill he discovered at Lane Theological Seminary:

> But in all respects I am treated just as kindly, and as much like a brother by the students, as if my skins as white, and my education as good as their own. Thanks to the Lord, prejudice against color does not exist in Lane

14. Bradley, "Brief Account," 688.
15. Bradley, "Brief Account," 689.

Theological Seminary. If my life is spared, I shall probably spend several years here, and prepare to preach the gospel.[16]

Having completed his story up to the point of its writing, Bradley addressed his greatest passions: the gospel of Jesus and liberation for his enslaved brothers and sisters. He spoke of an experience that transpired in 1828 where, after speaking with Christians concerning his soul, he was led to the cross of Christ and "oh how I longed to be able to read the Bible."[17] Bradley got an old spelling book, which he kept in his hat and, when he would get up in the night to work, he would read from the Bible. Bradley recounted a time when he persuaded one of his young masters to teach him to write, but the second night of lessons his "mistress came in, bustled about, scolded her son, and called him out. I overheard her say to him, 'You fool! What are you doing? If you teach him to write, he will write himself a pass and run away.'"[18] Even so, Bradley persisted in his studies until he was able to teach himself to write.

Having written of his passion for the gospel of Jesus, Bradley now closed his letter to the *Oasis* by describing his desire for freedom. During Bradley's time as a slave, there were all forms of propaganda created by those who would seek to defend slavery and extend its reach. Among these forms of propaganda was the advancement of the idea that there are slaves who actually wished to remain enslaved and did not long to be free. Bradley, using similar language he artfully employed in the debates at Lane Theological Seminary just four months prior to writing to the *Oasis*, wrote the following argument: "How strange it is that anybody should believe any human being could be a slave, and yet be contented. I do not believe there ever was a slave who did not long for liberty."[19] Bradley delivered an impassioned conclusion on the matter, declaring,

16. Bradley, "Brief Account," 689.
17. Bradley, "Brief Account," 689.
18. Bradley, "Brief Account," 689.
19. Bradley, "Brief Account," 689.

James Bradley and the Lane Rebels

> The truth is, if a slave shows any discontent, he is sure to be treated worse, and worked harder for it; and every slave knows this. This is why they are careful not to show any uneasiness when White men ask them about freedom. When they are alone by themselves, all their talk is about liberty—liberty! It is the great thought and feeling that fills the minds full all the time.[20]

Upon sharing the account of his life and his perspective on the slave's desire for freedom, Bradley closed his autobiographical account in the tradition of the great seminarians from centuries gone by who had paved the way before him:

> I could say much more; but as your letter requested a "short account" of my life, I am afraid I have written too much already. I will say but a few words more. My heart overflows when I hear what is doing for the poor broken-hearted slave, and free men of color. God will help those who take part with the oppressed. Yes, blessed be his holy name! He will surely do it. Dear Madam, I do hope I shall meet you at the resurrection of the just. God preserve you, and strength you in this holy cause, until the walls of prejudice are broken down, the chains burst in pieces, and men of every color meet at the feet of Jesus, speaking kind words, and looking upon each other in love—willing to live together on earth, as they hope to live in eaven![21]

Bradley's account offers clarifying insight into the experiences and motives that drove his participation with the rest of those at Lane Theological Seminary who later were to be known as the "Lane Rebels." Blassingame described the outright necessity of firsthand accounts to gain perspective and understanding, noting that students "should always remember the observation of Frederick Douglass that a free man 'cannot see things in the same light with the slave, because he does not, and cannot, look from

---

20. Bradley, "Brief Account," 690.
21. Bradley, "Brief Account," 690.

the same point from which the slave does."[22] Blassingame aptly concluded,

> The individual and collective mentality of the slaves, the ways they sought to fulfill their needs, the experiential context of life in the quarters and in the fields, and the black man's personal perspective of bondage emerge only after an intensive examination of the testimony of slaves and former slaves.[23]

JAMES BRADLEY ARRIVES AT LANE

Upon reflecting on his arrival and opportunity to learn as a student in the classroom, Bradley described his time at Lane Theological Seminary with gratitude and charity; he recalled being treated "just as kindly and as much like a brother by the students, as if my skins as white, and my education as good as their own."[24] Having experienced some of the worst of human behavior rooted in racist hatred and violence for the entirety of his life up until arriving at Lane Theological Seminary, Bradley now found a home where, in his own words, "prejudice against color does not exist."[25]

If this was true of the students at Lane Theological Seminary, it seems that it was also true of many of the faculty and administration there as well. A contemporary of Bradley's and fellow student Huntington Lyman later recalled that even their exit from the seminary did not "infract the reverence and love which we bore to the reverend men, Beecher, Stowe, and Morgan of the faculty. We were attached to these teachers by bonds that have yielded to no gentle strain."[26] In stark contrast to the welcome he received on the shores of Charleston, James Bradley's first days at Lane were characterized

---

22. Blassingame, *Slave Testimony*, lxv.
23. Blassingame, *Slave Testimony*, lxv.
24. Bradley, "Brief Account," 689.
25. Bradley, "Brief Account," 689.
26. Lyman, "Rebels," 61.

by hospitality and love. It is no surprise that Bradley recalled his days at Lane Theological Seminary with such gratitude.

Lyman Beecher, the seminary's first president in 1832, was committed to making Bradley feel as welcome as any other student despite being the only Black student at the institution. Lane historian Lawrence Thomas Lesick remarked of the President that "Beecher himself had no objection to the commixture of the races; after a social gathering for the students at his home he expressed regret that James Bradley had felt it best not to attend."[27] Beecher was known as a man of high ideals and good intentions, but ideals and intentions mean little when they are not substantiated by meaningful action; Beecher's inaction would later be a critical turning point in the story of the seminary over which he presided.

THE HISTORY OF LANE THEOLOGICAL SEMINARY

Lyman Beecher was trained for ministry at Yale, graduating from the Divinity School in 1798. He spent the next thirty-four years in various forms of pastoral ministry while raising thirteen children. When Ebenezer and William Lane pledged four thousand dollars for a new Presbyterian school near Cincinnati in 1829, Beecher was tapped to be its first president. Beecher was elected in 1830 as both president and professor of theology but did not begin his role with the newly-formed institution until 1832.

The rapid expansion of the young country to the western territories instilled a sense of urgency for those who sought to evangelize the masses. In 1829, Cincinnati was one of many western cities that drew the attention of benefactors such as Ebenezer and William Lane who wanted to establish a theological training ground for ministers of the gospel who would ensure adherence to moral standards and advance the cause of God's kingdom in the city of Cincinnati and beyond. At the time of Lane Theological Seminary's founding, an article was published in the *Cincinnati*

---

27. Lesick, *Lane Rebels*, 95.

Pandect on Tuesday, September 8, 1829, describing the impetus for this great cause. The article began with a celebratory tone: "We rejoice in being permitted to lay before you at this interesting season, the rise, progress, plan, and designs of an institution which claims the highest consideration of every enlightened citizen."[28] The *Cincinnati Pandect* article goes on to describe the seminary as "worthy of support of every friend of Science, Literature, and Religion."[29] In describing the founding purpose for the seminary, the article recorded it as an institution to "promote the interests of the Redeemer's Kingdom and produce the greatest amount of good."[30]

The *Cincinnati Pandect* reported that as part of the original plan for the new seminary, students "shall be required to spend a certain portion of time in manual labor, in farming or the mechanics."[31] One of the first documents describing the Charter of Lane Theological Seminary and Walnut Hills School delineated tuition and board charges at a grand total of fifty dollars per year for students in the Theological Department. The curriculum at the seminary was intentionally designed for students to be able to have enough time to work in Cincinnati in concert with their theological training so they could pay for their education and prepare for full-time vocational ministry simultaneously. The charter recorded the standards for admission:

> As no young men are received into the Institution, but those who produce satisfactory testimonials of good moral character, as a large majority of the students are hopefully pious; and as all our instructors, will make it a primary object to protect and elevate the moral character of their pupils; the Board believe that parents may send their sons to this Institution, without the painful

---

28. *Cincinnati Pandect*, September 8, 1829, 1.
29. *Cincinnati Pandect*, September 8, 1829, 1.
30. *Cincinnati Pandect*, September 8, 1829, 1.
31. *Cincinnati Pandect*, September 8, 1829, 1.

apprehension that their moral character will be corrupted or destroyed.[32]

In addition to President Beecher, the founders also persuaded Calvin Stowe to come to Cincinnati and serve as professor of biblical literature. Later, Thomas Biggs and John Morgan also joined as faculty members. The foundation of the seminary was only possible through the generosity of key donors along the way. One of these donors, a man by the name of Elnathan Kemper, along with his brothers, generously provided sixty acres of land on which were both the Walnut Hills School—that would serve as a preparatory school for Lane—and the seminary. The article published in the *Cincinnati Pandect* called for the financial support of others who shared the vision for a seminary in Cincinnati and declared that "in so doing, generations yet unborn will rise up and call you blessed, and a crown of rejoicing will be your rich reward."[33]

Shortly after Lane's establishment, a student enrolled whose influence on the campus would forever change the course of the young seminary at Walnut Hills. As a young man, Theodore Weld was greatly influenced by the religious zeal of the great American revivalist Charles Grandison Finney. Finney's spiritual fervor captured Weld's imagination and converted him to the cause of spreading the gospel into the burgeoning American West. Finney ardently encouraged the kind of spiritual transformation that causes one to not only change their ideology but move one toward action: lending their voice to the conversation and their hands to the good work of the Great Commission of Jesus Christ, advancing God's kingdom on Earth.

Finney's ardent zeal for the Lord touched every aspect of his thinking and living and the current issues of the day were not immune from this influence. Finney recounted coming to a place of personal conviction on the matter of slavery: "When I first went to New York, I had made up my mind on the question of slavery, and

---

32. Lane Theological Seminary, Charter and Amendments, para 3.
33. *Cincinnati Pandect*, September 8, 1829, 1.

was exceedingly anxious to arouse public attention to the subject."[34] Finney noted, "In my prayers and preaching, I so often alluded to slavery, and denounced it, that a considerable excitement came to exist among the people."[35] Committed to following Finney's lead, Theodore Weld was deeply moved by the anti-slavery work of the Scotsman, Charles Stuart. Having been moved to pursue piety and spiritual transformation, Weld now turned to lending his voice and his hands to the work of abolition. While Stuart had significant influence abroad, Fletcher noted, "The influence of Stuart in the history of American anti-slavery was chiefly felt through Weld."[36] Weld quickly rose through the ranks of those committed to the cause of abolition of the slave trade in America.

Theodore Weld was appointed as one of the first of four agents of the American Anti-Slavery Society in which he worked in partnership with brothers Arthur and Lewis Tappan to establish in 1831. While he acknowledged there was much work yet to be done in the east, Weld felt a strong call to go west, and in particular to Lane Theological Seminary, where a young group of seminarians might be persuaded to aid in advancing the cause of abolition in the western territories. Lane, like many similar institutions across the country, had a clear presence of the American Colonization Society on their campus. However, it did not yet have an apparent abolitionist counterpart. Therefore, Theodore Weld arrived on the scene in Cincinnati to be among the first to enroll at Lane Theological Seminary and begin to win the hearts and minds of his classmates for the cause of abolition of which he cared so deeply.

In antebellum America, it was not uncommon for institutions of higher education to be split in opinion—host to students who resided ideologically on either side of the colonization and abolition argument. Such was the case at Lane Theological Seminary and countless other institutions across the higher education landscape. Lane's founding came at a time of ubiquitous debate within the realm of American higher education on the most pressing

---

34. Finney, *Autobiography*, 295.
35. Finney, *Autobiography*, 295.
36. Fletcher, *History of Oberlin*, 151.

question of the day. In many ways, the academe led the conversation in response to the slavery question as the public turned its eyes and ears to the scholars of their day. In fact, Wilder argues that the "greatest domestic questions of the nineteenth century were debated in racial terms, and thus they enhanced the authority of the academy in political affairs."[37] During one of the most fractured times in American history, the faculty and students of its colleges and universities had a prominent voice in the ongoing debate. "Scholars acquired broad influence as they responded to anxieties about the makeup of the nation and crafted arguments for restricting membership in American society."[38]

THE SLAVERY QUESTION

Lyman Beecher arrived to the president's seat at Lane at a time when the winds of change were blowing wildly across antebellum America. The convicted consciences of many in higher education raised the volume on the moral imperative of abolition. Nevertheless, as is often the case, the enticing allure of self-preservation complicated matters as many of the first colleges and universities were economically sustained by the same slave trade that was being called into question. Wilder identified two substantial forces, the American Revolution and the Second Great Awakening, which had "incited a sincere and prolonged critique of slavery on campuses that remained financially dependent upon slave owners and slave traders."[39]

The efforts of zealous abolitionists aggravated those who believed that abolition would severely disrupt the composition of an expanding American society. Nonetheless, a "lively anti-slavery discourse flowered on the young nation's campuses."[40] Huntington Lyman, a Lane Theological Seminary student who would later

37. Wilder, *Ebony and Ivy*, 243.
38. Wilder, *Ebony and Ivy*, 243.
39. Wilder, *Ebony and Ivy*, 243.
40. Wilder, *Ebony and Ivy*, 243.

leave the institution alongside his fellow rebels, reflected years later on the historical moment in America into which Lane Theological Seminary was birthed. Lyman recalled,

> The American Anti-Slavery Society had just been formed. Lundy and Garrison, like bulls rampant, were fretting the Northern welkin with their roar. The Southern sea was agitated as though the winds of heaven were surging upon it, while the "solid South" was whittling upon the ligaments that held Dixie to the Union.[41]

The two sides of the argument refused to give an inch to the other as the debates raged throughout the country. The Reverend Jonathan Edwards Jr., who would go on to preside over Union College, "charged that the slave trade had brought only brutality, inhumanity, bloodshed, warfare, upheaval, and immorality to Africa, Europe, and the Americas."[42] The argument of the American Colonization Society was not to rationalize the morality of the slavery, rather its proponents sought to make the case that it was in the best interests of slaves to return to their homeland of Africa. Many slaves, including James Bradley, spoke out against the colonization plan. Some historians maintain that colonization was, in essence, merely a compromise that aided Christians in their desire to wash their hands of slavery while also preserving the privileges of power in an increasingly heterogeneous society.

The American Colonization Society had established the college campus as the ideal location to spread their ideology and, at the time Lane Theological Seminary was established in Cincinnati, there were active colonization societies on three-fifths of the approximately sixty colleges in the free states. When the American Anti-Slavery Society was established in 1831, these college campuses became the primary battleground. Abolitionists were viewed by the American Colonization Society as "dangerous advocates of a multiracial future."[43] Student abolitionists met

---

41. Lyman, "Rebels," 61.
42. Wilder, *Ebony and Ivy*, 244.
43. Wilder, *Ebony and Ivy*, 266.

James Bradley and the Lane Rebels

resistance at nearly every turn. Oberlin historian J. Brent Morris posited, "Indeed, conservatives in academia had made it nearly impossible for progressive young students to pursue their education unencumbered."[44] Examples of such resistance could be found all across higher education in America. North of Lane Theological Seminary in Hudson, Ohio, Western Reserve College organized the first affiliate organization of the American Anti-Slavery society on the campus prompted by the encouragement of President Charles B. Storrs and Professor Elizur Wright Junior. Theodore Weld also visited Western Reserve at this time prior to the debates at Lane Theological Seminary. The abolitionists on campus many times were faced with the difficult proposition of not only convincing their fellow students—many who came from slave-owning families, but doing so on campuses where the administration made it abundantly clear where they and the rest of the campus leadership stood on the matter.

What transpired at Western Reserve happened repeatedly in various manifestations of the abolitionist spirit in students and faculty. Further east in Whitestown, New York, the President of Oneida Institute, Beriah Green, established an anti-slavery society as well. In many cases, when abolitionists went to work in the communities surrounding their campuses, they were met with great resistance; not only from many of the wealthier and influential community members but also through the pages of the local press. As the abolitionist wave swelled, an editorialist for *Western Monthly Magazine* made a universal plea that colleges "belonged to the public, and nothing abrasive to the public harmony or divisive in civil affairs could be tolerated in the curriculum or the culture of the student body."[45] In many cases, the American Colonization Society was presented as an appropriate option for college students to support, while the more zealous cause of abolition was labeled divisive, disharmonious, and blatantly wrong.

One of the prominent cases of colonization and abolitionism debate transpired in the heart of one of the more established

---

44. Morris, *Hotbed of Abolitionism*, 38.
45. Wilder, *Ebony and Ivy*, 267.

colonial states in Amherst, Massachusetts. The controversy began when the Amherst College administration refused to allow abolitionist Arnold Buffum to come to the campus. The administration would later double down in their efforts in 1834 by attempting to end any and all discussions of the slavery matter, just as the administration at Lane Theological Seminary would do later in the same year. The efforts of President Humphrey to mute the students' abolitionist fervor did not hinder the students from continuing to meet, so the Board and Administration devised a plan to implement rules that would severely restrict the anti-slavery society, rules that would eventually cause its death.

These types of battles between students and administration were happening all across the young country. In Hanover, Indiana, the public became aware of a clandestine anti-slavery society among the students and put enormous pressure on the President James Blythe to put such nonsense to an end. Blythe, who was himself a slaveholder, "insisted that the public affairs of the nation had no place on campus."[46] Rather, the primary role of the student from the perspective of Blythe was simple and could be summed up in one word: Obey. Similar situations with eerily similar events played out at Hamilton College, Marietta College, and Miami College. Hamilton College students prayed that not only their campus but also every institution of American higher education would truly examine the question of slavery. Concurrently, anti-slavery societies were established at Colby College, Union College, and Dartmouth.

In nearly all of these cases, the administration, faculty, and local communities sought to silence the students' zeal. In some circumstances, the students ultimately acquiesced to the bidding of administration in order to remain in good standing with the college. However, in many other contexts the students could not in good conscience give up their fight. Instead, they chose various forms of protest in carrying their cause forward. At Phillips Andover, twenty-five miles north of Boston, fifty students chose to leave the academy instead of complying with the institutional

---

46. Wilder, *Ebony and Ivy*, 269.

mandate to cease meeting as an anti-slavery society. Galvanized by the powerful development of standing against authority for a cause they believed in, many of these students would remain active in the abolitionist cause throughout their lives.

The decision to hold steady to their abolitionist conviction was not an easy one. Individuals and institutions that identified themselves as sympathetic to slaves and advocates of abolition were often the targets of malicious violence. The riots in New York in July of 1834 ransacked a theatre and proceeded with the declared intent that the "hanging of an abolitionist would finish off the night's pleasure."[47] Who was the target of their hatred? None other than Arthur Tappan who, alongside his brother Lewis, provided financial support toward meeting the Lane Theological Seminary Rebels' conditions at Oberlin College. With torches lit, the mob came to Lewis's home first and set it ablaze.

Riots inciting violence against abolitionists were far too familiar for those who held such a conviction. Noyes Academy in New England opened their doors to students of both genders and students of all races in Canaan, New Hampshire, in 1835. In direct response, a "mob of three hundred people hunted Black students with guns and a cannon, then used oxen and horses to pull the academy's building from its foundations and drag it through town."[48] Amherst also experienced violent outbursts in response to the anti-slavery movement that had been undertaken. Wherever the abolitionist cause was advanced, it seemed that violence was sure to follow.

A rising tide of forces stood against the cause of abolitionists even in the free state of Ohio. The lawmakers who had "opposed slavery for racist reasons set the policy tone in early Ohio and did everything in their power to keep free African Americans out."[49] Laws that would later be known an infamy as "Black Laws" were passed in 1804 and 1807. Within the letter of these Black Laws were enormous restrictions on would-be Black citizens of

---

47. Asbury, "Abolition Riots," 1.
48. Wilder, *Ebony and Ivy*, 271–72.
49. Morris, *Hotbed of Abolitionism*, 28.

Ohio. Although it was ostensibly a free state by rule of law, those in power over the state were emboldened to take whatever measures necessary in order to prevent a multiracial society in Ohio. Included in the Black Laws were decrees that "required two White sponsors and a prohibitive bond of five hundred dollars for African Americans to enter the state, barred them from militia service, and denied them the right to testify against Whites in court or to vote."[50] In the face of these seemingly insurmountable odds, James Bradley crossed the Ohio River and not only settled in the state of Ohio, but also began studies at an institution that did not have a policy for his acceptance. The remarkable nature of these achievements is difficult to overstate.

The violent repercussions that often accompanied the slavery debate stoked the fears of White leaders to do anything that might advance the cause of abolition. At Lane Theological Seminary, the members of the Board of Trustees were Cincinnati business executives who were deeply disturbed by the idea of seminary students getting involved in the public debate surrounding slavery. The students, in the mind of the trustees, were there for the sole purpose of preparing for ministry and any activity connected to the issue of slavery was simply a distraction. Fletcher recounted that the "race feeling was strong in the city; the riots of five years before had not been forgotten, clearly they [the Board of Trustees] could not afford to have their names associated with an institution . . . publicly identified with abolitionism."[51]

PRELUDE TO THE DEBATES

The Lane Board of Trustees would have been all too familiar with the volatile nature of race relations in antebellum Cincinnati. "Cincinnati racial violence dates back to 1829, when Whites drove about one thousand African Americas—or half of the city's Black

---

50. Morris, *Hotbed of Abolitionism*, 28.
51. Fletcher, *History of Oberlin*, 155.

James Bradley and the Lane Rebels

population—out of town."[52] In 1829, the number of Black citizens in Cincinnati rose to 2,258, which was substantially higher than the previous census of 620 in 1826. The Black population was now approximately 10 percent of the city. Threatened by the growing population, mobs of Whites relentlessly attacked.

The Lane Board of Trustees saw the emerging Seminary as a refuge from public discourse and sought to protect their own interests in having their names associated with the institution. It is unknown how the Board reacted to the arrival of students like James Bradley, Theodore Weld, James Thome, and others; however, it was not long before their influence was felt by all associated with the seminary. Weld arrived at Lane Theological Seminary and began to set the stage for a public discussion on slavery at Lane to be held in February of 1834.

President Beecher quickly took note of Weld's ability to capture the hearts and minds of his fellow students. In fact, from Beecher's estimation of the student perspective, Theodore Weld very well may have been considered the President of the institution. Beecher described Weld's influence: "In the estimation of the class Theodore Weld was president—he took the lead of the whole institution . . . they thought he was a god."[53] As he had done along previous stops in his fervent campaign for abolition, Weld sought allies, appealed to the hearts of the institutional leadership, and stood ready to challenge those who would give a defense to the central tenets of colonization. Weld spread the word across the small campus at Walnut Hills that he intended to instigate a public debate on the question of slavery to begin in February of 1834. Just a year following the initiation of these campus-wide debates, a large portion of those who would participate would be beginning a new chapter at Oberlin Collegiate Institute.

In tracing the history of the abolition of slavery in America, many important names and places ought to be remembered. The small town and college of Oberlin, Ohio, should be mentioned in the same company as many of its larger peers. "Oberlin was,

---

52. Kiesewetter, "Civil Unrest."
53. Fletcher, *History of Oberlin*, 151.

The Light of Knowledge

beyond question, one of the most important communities in the abolitionist movement. In its symbolic and practical importance, it rivaled larger and more well-known eastern reform centers."[54] The size and scope of these abolitionist actions were embodied by men and women whose character and conviction abundantly overshadowed the size and scope of the town limits of this small Midwestern community.

How does such a thing transpire? How does a small and seemingly inconsequential college in a small and seemingly inconsequential town have such a profound impact on a decisive movement in American history? The answers to these questions trace their roots, in part, to a zealous group of students gathering over the course of eighteen February nights in Cincinnati to win the hearts and minds of a campus on the imperative question of their day.

---

54. Morris, *Hotbed of Abolitionism*, 2.

Chapter 3

THE DEBATES AT LANE THEOLOGICAL SEMINARY

THE PERFECT STORM

THE CONDITIONS AT LANE Theological Seminary in 1834 were conducive to a perfect storm. In the heat of the anti-slavery discussion, academic freedom was an endangered species on college campuses. Fletcher posited, "It is not surprising the great test should have come at Lane Theological Seminary, for there was gathered an unusually mature and serious-minded group of students, led by a genius and inspired by the greatest preacher of the day."[1] Fletcher's reflection underscores the importance of Theodore Weld's arrival on Lane's campus and the many ways Finney's preaching had served as an inspiration for Weld's actions. Despite the growing influence of abolitionists like Weld, Lane Theological Seminary, like many other similar institutions at the time, was comprised of students who were fully versed on both sides of abolition and colonization arguments.

The complicated nature of the seminary at Walnut Hills begins with its geography. Lane Theological Seminary, being situated only a stone's throw away from a slave state, drew students who

1. Fletcher, *Hotbed of Abolitionism*, 150.

had not only heard stories of slavery, many also had firsthand experience. Some students came from slave-owning families and even owned slaves themselves. Huntington Lyman described the impetus for the debates as one where "the outgoing of our ethical inquiries brought us to this very theme—slavery."[2] Though many students had some experience with the matter, the public rhetoric had left a general sense of indecision on the matter. Lyman posited, "I suppose there was a general consent in the institution that slavery was somehow wrong and to be got rid of. There was not a readiness to pronounce it a sin."[3]

Due to the fact the colonization society was allowed to stand with no opposition, the students petitioned President Beecher to have the debates. Beecher somewhat begrudgingly granted permission despite the protest of one faculty member, Thomas Biggs. Despite the protest offered by Biggs, not only did Beecher ultimately grant permission for the meetings, he even chose to attend some of the discussion and submitted a written statement on his perspective to be read aloud to those gathered. Biggs spoke openly about his disproval of the proceedings, but against his advice, the students announced their plan to begin the debates on February 5, 1834, and may have even had their first meeting that same night.

To give appropriate balance in setting the stage for the debates, the students gathered as much information as possible from the perspectives of both sides of the discussion through the circulation of pre-reading material across the campus. One of the Lane students, H. B. Stanton, reported,

> We possessed all the numbers of the African Repository, from its commencement, nearly all the Annual Reports of the Colonization Society, and the prominent documents of the Anti-Slavery Society. In addition to the above, our kind friends in the city furnished us with Colonization pamphlets in profusion. Dr. Shane, a young gentleman of Cincinnati, who had been out to Liberia, with a load of emigrants, as an agent of the Colonization

2. Lyman, "Rebels," 62.
3. Lyman, "Rebels," 62.

Society, furnished us with a long statement concerning the colony; and a distinguished instructress, recently of Hartford, Connecticut, now of Cincinnati, sent us communication from her hand, which attempted to prove that Colonizationists and Abolitionists ought to unite their efforts, and not contend against one another. These were our materials. And, sir, it was emphatically a discussion of facts, facts, *facts*.[4]

The discussion of facts as Stanton described was a dialogue that involved nearly every single individual on the Lane Theological Seminary campus. In fact, the entirety of the student body and the full faculty with the exception of Thomas Biggs attended the debates. This free discussion on the issue of slavery took place on campus during the evenings after classes were completed for the day. Two questions were selected to initiate the conversation that ultimately carried a total of nine evenings for two and a half hours each, producing approximately forty-five total hours of dialogue over the course of those cold February nights in southern Ohio. The two questions that framed the debates were recorded by Stanton as follows,

> Ought the people of the Slaveholding States to abolish Slavery immediately?
> Are the doctrines, tendencies, and measures of the American Colonization Society, and the influence of its principal supporters, such as render it worthy of the patronage of the Christian public?[5]

Nine nights were dedicated to answering the question of immediate abolition, and nine nights were dedicated to the central tenets of colonization. Over the course of the eighteen nights, there would be seventeen different speakers. Stanton described the lineup of speakers accordingly, "Nearly half of the seventeen speakers . . . were the sons of slaveholders; one had been a slaveholder himself; one had till recently been a slave; and the residue

---

4. Stanton, "Great Debate," 3.
5. Stanton, "Great Debate," 3.

were residents of, or had recently traveled or lived in slave states."[6] Prior to each point to be discussed, all participants took time to consider all the documentation, and they were careful to hear from two people on each point, one from each side.

Having cultivated the ground at Lane Theological Seminary for some time leading up to the commencement of the debates, Theodore Weld took the stage first, opening the debate "with a series of powerful lectures in favor of immediate emancipation."[7] Lyman recalled that the evening debates were equally long and earnest. Despite the length and intensity of the discussion, there was an irenic spirit among the students. "All the fire of the contest entered into the local discussion, but without its bitterness."[8] Lyman posited, "Knowledge upon the subject was short and crude. There was, however, a single exception . . . Weld—and when he came to speak he held the floor for eighteen hours."[9] Weld's influence on the campus offered him a place of authority, earned, from the perspective of the administration or not, among his fellow seminarians.

Five years after the debates at Lane Theological Seminary, Theodore Weld wrote the following in the introduction to his book, *American Slavery as It Is*; it is not difficult to imagine that his opening remarks at the seminary had remarkable similarities:

> Reader, you are empaneled as a juror to try a plain case and bring in an honest verdict. The question at issue is not one of law, but of fact—"What is the actual condition of the slaves in the United States?" A plainer case never went to jury. Look at it. Twenty-seven hundred thousand persons in this country, men, women, and children, are in slavery. Is slavery, as a condition for human beings, good, bad, or indifferent? We submit the question without argument. You have common sense, and conscience, and a human heart; pronounce upon it. You have a wife, or a husband, a child, a father, a mother,

6. Stanton, "Great Debate," 3.
7. Fletcher, *History of Oberlin*, 152.
8. Lyman, "Rebels," 62.
9. Lyman, "Rebels," 62.

a brother or a sister—make the case your own, make it theirs, and bring in your verdict. The case of Human Rights against Slavery has been adjudicated in the court of conscience times innumerable. The same verdict has always been rendered—"Guilty"; the same sentence has always been pronounced, "Let it be accursed." . . . There is not a man on earth who does not believe that slavery is a curse. Human beings may be inconsistent, but human nature is true to herself. She has uttered her testimony against slavery with a shriek ever since the monster was begotten; and till it perishes amidst the execrations of the universe, she will traverse the world on its track, dealing her bolts upon its head, and dashing against it her condemning brand. We repeat it, every man knows that slavery is a curse. Whoever denies this, his lips libel his heart. Try him; clank the chains in his ears, and tell them they are for *him*. Give him an hour to prepare his wife and children for a life of slavery. Bid him make haste and get ready their necks for the yoke and their wrists for the coffle chains, then look at his pale lips and trembling knees, and you have *nature's* testimony against slavery.[10]

Under Weld's direction and influence, this resolute group of college students organized meetings devoted to the slavery question that would not only capture the attention of an entire campus but an entire city, in fact, an entire nation. Artful and articulate, Weld opened the debates with four potent speeches in total. Over the course of the ensuing evenings, a host of others shared eyewitness testimony of the gruesome realities of slavery. The eyewitnesses were not only passive observers of the atrocities of slavery; some had also been active participants in preserving its influence. The arrangement of these speakers, those who bore witness to the horrific reality of slavery, played a pivotal role in swaying the opinions of those who had gathered for the debates.

10. Weld, *American Slavery*, 7.

The Light of Knowledge

THE TESTIMONY OF JAMES BRADLEY

Of critical importance among those who spoke during these debates was James Bradley. Bradley recounted his personal testimony of being ripped away from his family and brought over from Africa on a slave ship; he was subsequently sold to a planter in South Carolina who would later settle in the Arkansas territory. When his master died, Bradley was able to work and buy his freedom. In 1833, longing for the power of a formal education, Bradley came to Lane Theological Seminary and was admitted into the academic department there.

While there were multiple key characters and many pivotal moments in the story of the hallowed Lane debates, the testimony of James Bradley stands as perhaps the single most decisive moment in turning the tide for the cause of abolition at Lane. Even though Bradley spoke far less than Theodore Weld and the many others who also participated, more of James Bradley's words have been preserved in the historical records over time than any other speaker in the debates. Furthermore, no other moment in the debates has been attributed with as much sentiment, as eyewitnesses speak of the full range of human emotion, from the room filling with roaring laughter to the presence of tears filling every listener's eyes when Bradley finished his moving testimony. Having been oppressed by the throes of slavery only weeks before this opportunity came to being and despite being the only Black student at Lane Theological Seminary, James Bradley commanded the attention of all in the room. In a matter of moments, Bradley captured and won the hearts and minds of all in attendance for the cause of abolition. The verdict was clear.

Bradley's testimony came toward the end of the portion of the debates related specifically to the first question: Ought the people of the Slaveholding States to abolish Slavery immediately? Bradley's published autobiography in the *Oasis* gives a glimpse of some of the contents of his personal eyewitness testimony on the atrocities of the slave trade. Stanton recalled, "James Bradley, the emancipated slave above alluded to, addressed us nearly two hours;

The Debates at Lane Theological Seminary

and I wish his speech could have been heard by every opponent of immediate emancipation to wit."[11] Bradley cunningly designed counterarguments to two of the key opinions of the colonization side: first, that it would be unsafe to the community to give freedom to Blacks, and secondly, that the condition of emancipated negroes would be worse than it is now as "they are incompetent to provide for themselves, that they would become paupers and vagrants, and would rather steal than work for wages."[12]

In addressing the first argument that emancipation would be a threat to the safety of the community, Bradley's artful reply stood in stark contrast to the dramatic caricatures of Black people that were often portrayed in the propaganda of the pro-slavery contingency. As he would later write in his autobiographical piece, Bradley spoke of the two great desires of all slaves, liberty and education. Stanton recalled Bradley's description of a slave's desire for freedom as a "heaven-born desire" that was "tramped in the dust by a free and Christian nation."[13]

Next, as a counter to the second argument that slaves are simply too incompetent to fend for themselves and that they would resort to violence and stealing as opposed to honest work, Bradley offered a reply bursting with entertaining sarcasm. Stanton recounted a room filled with laughter from both sides of the debate. Morris aptly captured the moment: "If slaves could take care of themselves as slaves, with the weight of supporting themselves and their masters on their shoulders, Bradley reasoned, 'strange if they couldn't do it when it tumbled off.'"[14]

The colonization side sought to disseminate the pervasive myths that had permeated the country that Black people are by nature less competent than Whites to think, act, and live responsibly in this newly formed republic. Bradley's words were powerful, but perhaps even more potent was Bradley's presence. His ability to command the room and successfully prosecute and expose the

11. Stanton, "Great Debate," 4.
12. Stanton, "Great Debate," 4.
13. Stanton, "Great Debate," 4.
14. Morris, *Hotbed of Abolitionism*, 25.

weak colonization arguments destroyed what remained of long-held myths. Bradley's witness offered a compelling counternarrative to what was all-too-commonly presented by those in power. Upon reflection of Bradley's testimony, Stanton recalled the presence that Bradley displayed:

> This shrewd and intelligent Black cut up these White objections by the roots, and withered and scorched them under the sun of sarcastic argumentation, for nearly an hour, to which the assembly responded in repeated and spontaneous roars of laughter, which were heartily joined in by both colonizationists and abolitionists. Do not understand me as saying that his speech was devoid of argument. No. It contained sound logic, enforced by apt illustrations. I with the slanderers of Negro intellect could have witnessed this unpremeditated effort.[15]

Stanton continued by recounting a brief summary of Bradley's journey to Lane Theological Seminary as he noted that he was taken from Africa "when an infant, and sold into slavery. His master, who resided in Arkansas, died, leaving him to his widow. He was then about eighteen years of age. For some years, he managed the plantation for his mistress."[16] Stanton described the terms of Bradley purchasing his freedom and was careful to note that, "Every cent of this money, $855, he earned by labor and trading."[17] Stanton's recollection of every financial detail of Bradley's path to freedom is telling of just how much Bradley's story had affected his fellow students. Conceivably more telling, however, was the substance of Stanton's final sentence on Bradley's story: "He is a beloved and respected member of this institution."[18] "Beloved" and "respected" were not terms often used when speaking of emancipated slaves in antebellum America. Bradley's courage through multiple near-death experiences and his yearning for education and liberty had contributed to a significant change in the hearts

15. Stanton, "Great Debate," 4.
16. Stanton, "Great Debate," 4.
17. Stanton, "Great Debate," 4.
18. Stanton, "Great Debate," 4.

and minds of his listeners in regard to how emancipated slaves ought to be viewed.

Bradley's moment in the debates was the key moment in stimulating the abolition argument. "The Lane students agreed with James Bradley, a Black seminarian who had been kidnapped into slavery directly from Africa, that the scheme was patently outrageous and offensive."[19] Morris described Bradley's impact:

> Despite the fact that "even Liberty" was bitter to him while anyone remain in bondage, he articulated his refusal to submit to any emigration scheme and leave his "brethren under the yoke." Thanks in no small part to the skill of Bradley, who are least one observer grouped with the most skilled abolitionists and who could "not be equaled by the more logical and polished of our Birney and Weld," the colonization debate ended with a similar result as the first.[20]

In similar fashion, another key historian of the Lane Debates, Lawrence Lesick, pointed to Bradley's testimony within the debates as a moment that stands above the rest in solidifying the position of the abolitionists. Lesick described Bradley's testimony as "the most moving account of the evils of slavery and the ability of Blacks to overcome those obstacles."[21] Lesick suitably summarized the moment: "For an hour Bradley described the earnest desires of all slaves for liberty and education. In recounting Bradley's comments fifty years later, George Clark wrote, 'I doubt there was a dry eye in the chapel.'"[22]

STRUCTURE AND CONTENT

In sum, the debates had the rapt attention of the seminary for the better part of the month of February in 1834. In addition to the

19. Morris, *Hotbed of Abolitionism*, 25.
20. Morris, *Hotbed of Abolitionism*, 25.
21. Lesick, *Lane Rebels*, 80.
22. Lesick, *Lane Rebels*, 80–81.

critical testimony and articulate argument presented by James Bradley, the debates were arranged in such a fashion to elicit dialogue through an equal distribution of time and opportunity for both sides. One of the Lane Rebels, Huntington Lyman, recalled the atmosphere at the seminary prior to the debates: "The basal mischief was slavery. Slavery opened a crack which enlarged to a chasm."[23] Thus, in response to the growing chasm being felt by those who inhabited this small, collegial, faith-based institution, the students determined it right to seek to understand all sides in response to the slavery question. Lyman noted, "We deemed it important as a preliminary to our life task, that we should make ourselves acquainted with the moral wants and maladies of our times . . . no domestic question of the era basseted out with such prominence as slavery."[24]

Moreover, there is the issue of the students' religious fervor. The unique context of a seminary demanded that the students not only address the issue of slavery as an academic question to be answered but a theological dilemma to be resolved, with eternal implications. Lyman described the complexity when he recalled that the students' "ethical inquiries brought us to this very theme—slavery. I suppose there was general consent in the institution that slavery was somehow wrong and to be got rid of. There was not a readiness to pronounce it a sin."[25] Seeking understanding of both the ethical and theological ramifications of the slave trade in a fledgling country in search of firm grounding, the students resolved to meet until these matters could be settled at Lane Theological Seminary. Stanton recalled the debates commencing with opening arguments, which included a passionate monologue from Weld occupying nearly two evenings as he made his case, including facts pertaining to slavery and the need for immediate emancipation. Following Weld's dramatic opening, the floor was open for conclusions, inferences, and dissent.

23. Lyman, "Rebels," 61.
24. Lyman, "Rebels," 61.
25. Lyman, "Rebels," 62.

The Debates at Lane Theological Seminary

Next, the students turned their focus to the experience of slavery, yielding the floor to those who had firsthand knowledge and experience. Stanton noted that four of the remaining five evenings were devoted to "the recital of facts in regard to slavery, slaves, and slaveholders, gathered not from written documents, but from careful personal observation and experiences."[26] The shift from discussing slavery in theoretical terms to the reflections of those who had experienced its evil firsthand was a significant shift in the tone of the debates. As with many topics, slavery is an issue of which there is nothing quite as powerful as the lived experiences of those who have truly bore its burden. In reflection upon this portion of the debates, Stanton penned the following: "No class in the country have stronger social affections than slaves; nevertheless, the ties of a parent and child, husband and wife, brother and sister, are torn asunder by this bloody traffic."[27]

Despite the context of an institution of higher education, the debates seem to have often felt more like revival services than any academic exercise in the view of those who participated. Morris argued that this revival-like feeling might be attributed to the fact that many of these students at Lane Theological Seminary had been converted by Finney and were "well-versed in the workings of revivalism."[28] Accordingly, the revival-like debates were filled with the witness of the brutal nature of slavery. These testimonies became the centerpiece of arguments intended to address both the head and the heart. Morris offered a similar description of these witnesses as "those formerly entangled with slavery gave their own testimony of the barbarity of the system from personal experience and became some of the most effective speakers."[29]

Debates pertaining to slavery in that era were often reduced to academic discussions focused on economic or social ends. In contrast, these debates held the power of proximity. The authority of eyewitness testimony was discovered in the ability to describe

---

26. Stanton, "Great Debate," 4.
27. Stanton, "Great Debate," 4.
28. Morris, *Hotbed of Abolitionism*, 24–25.
29. Morris, *Hotbed of Abolitionism*, 24–25.

the atrocities of slavery as they really were. In writing about these powerful moments during the dialogue at Lane Theological Seminary, Morris noted that these individuals "presented their firsthand observations for all to consider: visions of bloody whips, cries of agony, and red-hot brands."[30]

In the final analysis, eyewitness testimonies in combination with the facts and persuasive arguments offered by Weld at the onset of the debates resulted in an overwhelming sentiment among the students for the cause of abolition. A unanimous vote fell in favor of immediate emancipation. The vote effectively brought the discussion on the first question to a close after nine nights of debates. The following evening the students gathered again to begin another nine-day debate to address the colonization question.

The debate of the second question, however, would not hold the same fervor of the nights that preceded it. Some of the students who had held convictions in favor of colonization had been deeply moved by the testimonies shared by fellow students during the first half of the debates. Stanton recalled one student who intended to take an active part, but "before he had an opportunity to take the floor, facts pressed upon him (he was always open to conviction) [and] he changed his views."[31] Stanton went on to record that not only did this student change his views, this student "left the institution for the purpose of commencing a school for the education of the people of color in Cincinnati, and has devoted himself to the elevation of free Blacks on our own soil."[32] When all was said and done, at the conclusion of the eighteen nights of free discussion on the matter, the Lane students were not only convicted of the moral and spiritual wrong of slavery, but they also felt deeply implicated toward its eradication in their immediate context. The result of the students' dialogue and reflection was a commitment to meaningful action toward the desired end of the immediate emancipation of every slave being held in bondage within the borders of the United States.

30. Morris, *Hotbed of Abolitionism*, 25.
31. Stanton, "Great Debate," 5.
32. Stanton, "Great Debate," 5.

IMMEDIATE AFTERMATH

The nature of the debates had not resulted in the expansion of the chasm that had previously existed at Lane Theological Seminary; rather, the dialogue produced a cohesive commitment and unity among the students. Many of these commitments to the abolition of slavery would not simply be a cause for a temporary act of student protest powered by the moment, rather a consuming passion over the course of many lifetimes. Stanton recalled "fears that there might be some unpleasant excitement, particularly as slaveholders, and prospective heirs to slave property, were to participate" in the debates—nonetheless, to Stanton's great surprise, "the kindest feelings prevailed. There was no crimination, no denunciation, no impeachment of motives."[33]

Stanton captured the sentiment of his fellow rebels at the conclusion of the debates when he noted that they were convinced that "prejudice is vincible, that colonization is vulnerable, and that immediate emancipation is not only right, and practicable, but is expedient."[34] Over the course of less than three weeks the thoughtful dialogue of the students had moved them from questioning the sinful nature of slavery to crying out, "Who will heed the cry of the oppressed?" In addition to what Stanton recalled, Lyman remembered the transformation in one student's life "who had come to the seminary relying upon the hire of his slaves to carry him through his theological course, went home and emancipated his slaves and put himself to expense for their benefit."[35] In similar fashion, another of the Lane Theological Seminary Rebels, James Thome, described the personal transformation he experienced through participation:

> Within a few months' residence at Lane, and by means of a discussion unparalleled in the brotherly feeling and fairness which characterized it, and the results which it brought out, the great principles of duty stood forth, sin

---

33. Stanton, "Great Debate," 5.
34. Stanton, "Great Debate," 5.
35. Lyman, "Rebels," 63.

revived, and I died. And, sir, though I am at this moment the heir to a slave inheritance, and though, forsooth, I am one of those unfortunate beings upon who slavery is by force entailed, yet I am bold to denounce the whole system as an outrage, a complication of crimes and wrongs, and cruelties that make angels weep.[36]

Resolved to take immediate action in the communities that surrounded the Lane Theological Seminary campus, the students began to consider the appropriate tactics. Fletcher noted, "Weld and his associates had no intention of fomenting slave insurrections nor of emancipating the slave through federal action."[37] The focus of the students' action was not in changing the legislation and laws, but first and foremost in changing hearts. Stanton articulated a strategy of reaching slaveholding communities by facts and arguments. The students' plan was to seek abolition and emancipation by appealing to slaveholders through a nationwide anti-slavery revival. The students were convinced "that if others could simply hear the truth of these matters and be presented with the facts, any human with a heart would join their cause of emancipation and abolition of the entire slave trade wherever it is found."[38]

Sustained by deep-seated conviction and motivated with a form of zeal that can only be found in the most optimistic student naivety, the students sought to achieve their mission and purpose not through traditional rebellion, but through the transformation of the human heart. Lyman wrote about the ironic nature of the "rebel" label that was later applied:

> The phrase, "Rebels of Lane Theological Seminary," is historic. There was no danger in the days of its origination, that it would convey a calumny; but the phrase survives while the events environed and explained it are forgotten. For this reason, it is of some consequence that I should say that it applies in a way of metaphorical

---

36. Stanton, "Great Debate," 7.
37. Fletcher, *History of Oberlin*, 153.
38. Fletcher, *History of Oberlin*, 154.

accommodation only. There was neither rebellion nor the shadow of rebellion in the event to which it points.[39]

The so-called rebellion was marked by gentleness. Moved by a commitment to Jesus Christ, of whom it was said, "a bruised reed he will not break, and a smoldering wick he will not snuff out," the students went about their work.[40] Fletcher concluded:

> Not by instigating the slaves to rebellion; Not by advocating an interposition of force on the part of the free states; Not by advocating congressional interference with the constitutional powers of the states; but by approaching the minds of the slave holders with the truth in the spirit of the Gospel.[41]

---

39. Lyman, "Rebels," 63.
40. Matthew 12:20., NIV.
41. Fletcher, *History of Oberlin*, 154.

Chapter 4

Trustees Upon the Stage

PECULIAR ACADEMIC PHENOMENON

FILLED WITH ABOLITIONIST ZEAL, the Lane students began their work in the city of Cincinnati. The students focused their initial efforts on providing education and opportunity to the Black community. In addition to education of children, the students also pursued the education of the elite, working tirelessly to win the hearts of those who maintained ties to the slave trade and those who worked for the cause of colonization within the city. The Board of Trustees at Lane Theological Seminary was comprised of men with substantial wealth and influence in the city of Cincinnati, and it was not long before they heard of the students' activities. The trustees quickly became concerned with the reputation of the seminary and the disruptive nature of the students' initiatives on their business relationships across the city of Cincinnati and beyond. As Huntington Lyman described it, "The faculty having dispersed, the trustees came upon the stage."[1]

Lyman and his fellow students felt as if they knew their teachers, but none of them would have been able to pick a member of the trustees from a lineup. Lyman described the trustees as elders who

---

1. Lyman, "Rebels," 63.

"seemed to regard us as mischievous boys, who needed additional bringing up. We were held to the seminary in part by necessity, much more by affection."[2] Upon reflection of the actions taken by the Board of Trustees, the students compared them to historical figures such as King Herod, Torquemada and his compeers in the Holy Office of the Inquisition, the Venetian Council of Ten, the Stuarts, and the Lord of the Star Chamber. Lyman recounted, "These are all who acted with total power when they thought it necessary to do so."[3]

Caught in the middle of the fervent students and the influential Board of Trustees was Lane Theological Seminary's president, Lyman Beecher. Beecher had been out of town for much of the time following the debates, traveling to raise financial support for the seminary. Lewis Tappan, who, along with his brother Arthur and their mutual friend Theodore Weld established the American Anti-Slavery Society and financially supported the founding of Oberlin College, recorded that Beecher returned to Lane Theological Seminary and "found that the trustees were resolute, the faculty fearful and undecided, and the students determined and unyielding."[4] Beecher's absence from the campus during the immediate aftermath of the Lane Debates would have a significant impact on the institutional response. "Beecher did not realize that the only one who could keep the seminary's friends from amplifying the evil was himself, and he left on a fund-raising trip to the East."[5]

Historian Robert Fletcher described the conditions as follows: "The threat came not from government but from conservative influences—chiefly business influences—which then, and so often later, have controlled that peculiar academic phenomenon, the unacademic 'Board of Trustees.'"[6] Unsurprisingly, the Lane Board of Trustees were immediately disturbed by the radical actions of

2. Lyman, "Rebels," 64.
3. Lyman, "Rebels," 64.
4. Tappan, *Life of Arthur Tappan*, 231.
5. Lesick, *Lane Rebels*, 95.
6. Fletcher, *History of Oberlin*, 150.

the student body, and the trustees felt they simply could not allow their good names to be connected to an institution that so overtly supported the cause of abolition.

One of the first shots at the Lane Theological Seminary students was taken in the form of an editorial published in the *Western Monthly Magazine*. The editorial's author, James Hall, compared the seminarians at Lane to boys in a grade school "wearing paper caps, flourishing wooden swords . . . but this is the first instance that we have ever known of a set of young gentlemen at school, dreaming themselves into full-grown patriots, and setting seriously to work, to organize a widespread revolution."[7] In the warm summer months of 1834, just months removed from the debates of February, the Lane Theological Seminary Board of Trustees organized. While President Lyman Beecher and the two faculty members who were sympathetic to the students' cause, Calvin Stowe and John Morgan, were away from the campus, the board members took immediate and impactful action.

Thomas Biggs was the one faculty member who had passionately spoke in protest to the students gathering to discuss the question of slavery. Biggs was convinced that the anti-slavery work of the students was antithetical to the educational purposes of the seminary. Biggs took his concerns to the Board of Trustees. A special sub-committee was appointed to determine what action should be taken. Biggs's sentiments regarding the anti-slavery society were scathing: "We are a reproach and a loathing in the land . . . that the offensive thing must be expurgated from the institution is my firm conviction."[8]

REPORT OF THE TRUSTEES

When the Lane Board of Trustees Executive Committee convened on August 20, 1834, they reviewed the report of the sub-committee and declared their position on the appropriateness of the

---

7. Fletcher, *History of Oberlin*, 156.
8. Fletcher, *History of Oberlin*, 157.

anti-slavery society on Lane Theological Seminary's campus in no uncertain terms. On the subject of slavery the Board of Trustees declared it to be "one of the deepest interest to all good citizens of these United States; yet which must always be approached with diffidence and discretion, for it has . . . thwarted the wisdom of the ablest and best men of the country."[9] The terms "diffidence" and "discretion" set a clear tone for the position of the trustees. It was evident, from their perspective, that this was a conversation meant only for the mature and not a matter to be discussed by students.

From the beginning, the trustees sought to put distance between the slavery debate and the matters of the seminary. The Board of Trustees argued that their remit was not to interfere in existing controversies; rather, "their concern is with the government of the Institution, and they would recommend no other measure than the interests of the usefulness of the institution."[10] While the students saw a clear connection between their theological studies and the question of slavery, the trustees delineated a clear line of distinction between the pious mission of the seminary and the social issues of the age. The students would never understand such a separation of theological instruction from theological conviction.

To justify their position, the trustees contended that the issue of slavery is one on which pious Christians differ. Accordingly, the seminary ought not to seek to be the arbiter of any controversial matter. The Board of Trustees maintained,

> For these, as well as other reasons . . . the Committee are of opinions, that everything tending to keep alive a spirit of controversy on the subject in question, ought to be excluded from the Seminary. The Committee are further of opinion that no associations or societies among the students ought to be allowed in the Seminary, except such as have for this immediate object improvement in the prescribed course of studies. They are of the opinion

---

9. Lane Board of Trustees, Meeting of Executive Committee, para 2.
10. Lane Board of Trustees, Meeting of Executive Committee, para 2.

that this society is particularly liable to some of the objections stated above and ought to be abolished.[11]

The matter was clear to the trustees. Discussions related to slavery had no place in the students' prescribed course of studies. While the students saw their abolitionist zeal as an outcome of their biblical studies, the trustees only saw a distraction—a distraction from the proper education of a seminary and, perhaps, a distraction directly affecting the reputation of those associated with Lane Theological Seminary. Consequently, on August 20, 1834, the trustees delivered five decisive resolutions to be considered by the full board and gave orders that a certificate copy of the proceedings of the day would be given directly to the members of the Lane Theological Seminary faculty.

The report of the trustees was published and distributed widely. The dissemination of the report assured that not only the Lane Theological Seminary students and faculty understood the position of the trustees, but also that the public would be confident of the administration's stance. The Board of Trustees reasoned that the location of the seminary—on the borders of a slave state— "calls for some peculiar cautionary measures in its government; and that the present state of public sentiment on some exciting topics requires restraints to be imposed, which under other circumstances might be entirely unnecessary."[12]

Among the many assumptions made by the trustees in rendering their decision, a few stood out to the students as particularly condescending. First, the trustees declared that they did not think the students could handle the magnitude of the discussion. In regard to the subject of slavery, the Board of Trustees contended that "its tendencies at this time are so obviously to absorb too much of the attention that the mind of the students can hardly can come in contact with it without injury."[13] Second, the administration's true concern for the reputation and financial prosperity of

---

11. Lane Board of Trustees, Meeting of Executive Committee, para 3.
12. Lane Board of Trustees, Meeting of Executive Committee, para 12.
13. Lane Board of Trustees, Meeting of Executive Committee, para 13.

the institution was thinly veiled. The Board of Trustees posited, "The Seminary is deeply implicated with one particular party and the slavery question and unless this impression can be removed, the prosperity of the Institution will be much retarded and its usefulness greatly diminished."[14] Third, the trustees invoked *in loco parentis* and took it upon themselves to care for the students as parents might look after their children. The Lane Board of Trustees declared, "It is due to the students and to those who entrust their children to the care of the Institution that the door should not be left open for employing such influences."[15]

Having re-established proper hierarchy of adults and children as it pertained to matters of the seminary, the sub-committee warned of the ramifications associated with allowing subordination. The Board of Trustees grouped the Lane Theological Seminary seminarians with other rebellious types eroding the foundation of the country: "It is evident to all who are accustomed to observe the signs of the times that there is at present in our country . . . a strong and growing propensity to insubordination . . . to justify resistance to law by private opinion."[16] The trustees painted the picture of midnight riots or public rebellion against the laws of the land. If such rebellion were to find its way even into a theological seminary, the Board of Trustees reasoned, "We may well despair of the republic"; after all, the Board of Trustees noted, "There is little danger in too much restraint."[17]

The executive committee of the trustees had left no doubt on their position on the matter, and their recommendations were heard across the campus and the city of Cincinnati. Put simply, the anti-slavery society was to be abolished and order was to be restored. Although they were only recommendations at the time, there was little doubt in the students' minds that the recommendations would be passed expediently. Plans were already being made by the students and faculty accordingly. Meanwhile, President

14. Lane Board of Trustees, Meeting of Executive Committee, para 13.
15. Lane Board of Trustees, Meeting of Executive Committee, para 14.
16. Lane Board of Trustees, Meeting of Executive Committee, para 16.
17. Lane Board of Trustees, Meeting of Executive Committee, para 16.

The Light of Knowledge

Lyman Beecher was hundreds of miles away in New York. Beecher had hoped to find some kind of compromise and even attempted to arrange for Theodore Weld to leave Lane Theological Seminary quietly. Unfortunately, Beecher had compounded the situation by agreeing to both support the trustees' decisions and also by promising to stand for the students' right to free discussion.

It was ironically at Beecher's home, without Beecher, on Monday, October 6, 1834, at 10 a.m., that the Lane Theological Seminary Board of Trustees gathered again to take action on the recommendations of the committee. The Lane Theological Seminary Board of Trustees reviewed the recommendations and with only three dissenting votes—Asa Mahan being one—passed two critical resolutions and two orders. The minutes of the Board of Trustees were recorded as follows: "Resolved that this Board approve and adopt the report of the sub-committee of the Executive Committee relative to the proceedings among the students on the subject of slavery and the proceedings of the executive committee."[18]

The first resolution passed by the trustees on October 6, 1834, was that societies of the students shall not be organized in the seminary. The second was that students shall not hold general meetings among themselves other than those of a religious or devotional character. The first put an effective end to the students' newly formed society and the second put precautionary measures to prevent anything like the February debates from transpiring again on the campus of Lane Theological Seminary.

The resolutions were potent enough, but it was the two orders of the executive committee that sounded the fall of the gavel. The Lane Theological Seminary Board of Trustees ordered:

> Whereas the anti-slavery society and the colonization society, lately organized in the Seminary, are considered by this board, in the present state of public excitement on the subject of slavery, as tending to enlist the students in controversies foreign to their studies, and to stir among themselves and in the community, unfriendly . . . and

18. Lane Board of Trustees, Meeting Minutes, para 1.

useless hostilities thereby counteracting the great objects of the Institution; Therefore ordered, that the students be required to discontinue those societies in the Seminary.

Ordered that the Executive Committee have power to dismiss any student from the Seminary when they shall think it necessary so to do; and to make rules and regulations for the admission of the students, or for the government and assuagement of the Seminary, or any of its concerns not inconsistent with the character and the regulations of this Board, which they may deem expedient.[19]

At its fundamental level, this was an issue of control. The seminary, as the board members advanced, belonged in neutral territory on such a divisive issue as slavery. Essentially, the Lane Theological Seminary Board of Trustees believed that the students were prematurely engaging in civil discourse and that such action was a distraction to what the administration deemed the pure motives and objectives of Lane Theological Seminary. The trustees made it abundantly clear that immediate action should be taken: namely, the immediate end of the anti-slavery society and a motion to dismiss William T. Allan.

Who was William T. Allan? Huntington Lyman recalled that he was highly regarded on campus, "most agreeable to his peers and to the faculty, son of an Alabama slaveholder, most scrupulous in the observance of every rule of the seminary . . . obnoxious only because he had been made president of our anti-slavery society."[20] Allan had no idea he was in the crosshairs of the Board's action. Lyman recorded Allan's predicament as follows: "There was Allan, asleep in his dormitory two miles away, while proceedings fatal to his character and to all his aspirations were proceeding in the office of a porkhouse in the city."[21]

Mercifully, the final action of these resolutions was postponed due to the absence of President Beecher. However, the gauntlet had

19. Lane Board of Trustees, Meeting Minutes, para 1.
20. Lyman, "Rebels," 65.
21. Lyman, "Rebels," 65.

been thrown to "sufficiently indicate to the students the course which the Trustees are determined to pursue."[22] Consequently, the board communicated their position through two resounding directives: relaying its intention to put an end to the anti-slavery society and firing Professor John Morgan, who was sympathetic to the students' cause.

ACQUIESCED IN ARBITRARY RULE

When President Lyman Beecher returned from New York, a trip that that had removed him from the seminary during its most pressing hour, he discovered a severely fractured campus. Tappan recalled that Beecher found that "the trustees were resolute, the faculty fearful and undecided, and the students determined and unyielding, repudiating the doctrine laid down by the trustees, and the 'order' based upon it."[23] Beecher quickly sought to do damage control with the students, advising them that this order from the Lane Theological Seminary Board of Trustees "might ere long be disregarded."[24] In doing so, Beecher woefully underestimated both the damage that had already been done and the unwavering resolve on the part of both the students and the Board of Trustees.

Nonetheless, much of the decisive action by the Board had already been levied in Beecher's absence. At their next meeting on October 10, 1834, the Lane Seminary Board of Trustees, in the absence of the seminary's president, ratified the action of the executive committee with a 14-to-3 vote. The board now held unrestricted power to dismiss any student from the seminary if they felt it necessary. The ostensible power of the trustees lacked force with the students. Many who had formed the anti-slavery society maintained a deeply rooted commitment to its sustained success. The students "were not children to be beaten into submission

---

22. Fletcher, *History of Oberlin*, 159.
23. Tappan, *Life of Arthur Tappan*, 231.
24. Tappan, *Life of Arthur Tappan*, 231.

Trustees Upon the Stage

to the pussy-footing tactics of their elders."[25] In response, James Thome declared that the students "will not only have their names, but their bodies cast out as evil, before they will hazard for one moment the cause of the oppressed, or yield an inch to the assaults of a corrupt and persecuting public sentiment."[26]

A deeply disturbed Board of Trustees in one corner and a profoundly resolute group of students in the other, a compromise seemed less and less likely with each passing day. President Lyman Beecher was now caught between assuaging the concerns of the Board and coming to the aid of his beloved students. The students held out hope that President Beecher was "ready to do everything in his power to keep in the seminary the group of brilliant young men of whom he was so justly proud."[27]

Beecher, however, would ultimately take a passive approach in addressing the entire matter. He was of the mind that all of this controversy would eventually subside and pass away in time. In the end, Beecher's failure to take decisive action played a pivotal role in the students' departure from the seminary. Less than twenty years later, the president's daughter, Harriet, would take much more decisive action for the cause of abolition in penning an anti-slavery novel, *Uncle Tom's Cabin*—a book that would play a significant role in laying the groundwork for civil war in the United States.

Tappan recalled the pivotal inaction of President Beecher:

> Dr. Beecher regretted the decision of the students, but he did not exercise the wisdom and firmness that the exigency required. He might have thrown himself into the breach, and said to the trustees, "I have never had such an opportunity; I cannot be separated from such 'noble men;' you must repeal the 'order,' or I shall feel constrained to put myself at the head of these students and lead them elsewhere." Had he done this, he might have saved the Seminary from the loss of such a band of moral heroes, and gained to himself a reputation beyond anything that he had previously acquired. But,

---

25. Fletcher, *History of Oberlin*, 159.
26. Fletcher, *History of Oberlin*, 159.
27. Fletcher, *History of Oberlin*, 161.

on the contrary, he acquiesced in the arbitrary rule of the trustees. A truly noble and fearless man in many respects, the opposition that prevailed at the seminary and throughout the country seemed to overcome him. Born to be a leader, under some circumstances, this eminent man failed at this time in an essential attribute of leadership of moral and religious enterprises.[28]

In addition to the frustrating inaction of their president, the students also felt deep disappointment with their faculty which had collectively issued a statement—also signed by President Beecher—on October 13, 1834, in which they declared that they saw nothing in the regulations being established by the Board of Trustees which is not common law in all well-regulated institutions. Saddened by the leadership of their beloved Seminary, the students resolved to prepare themselves to take the only action they felt that was left at their disposal—a mass exodus.

Once again, the students gathered to discuss all that had transpired and set a course of action to determine their collective next step. In the midst of their meetings, one of the student leaders stood up among those gathered and declared that he could no longer continue as a student at Lane Theological Seminary and that he would ask for an honorable dismission. The student leader proceeded to "request every student present, who was of the same mind and determination with himself, to signify the same by rising and standing upon his feet."[29]

On October 15, 1834, twenty-eight Lane Theological Seminary students presented a joint request for full dismission from the school, and the next day, eleven additional students did the same. The students' request for dismission was addressed to the faculty of Lane Theological Seminary and opened with the following statement: "The undersigned respectfully request that you will grant them a regular dismission from this institution."[30] The decision to leave Lane Theological Seminary was a difficult one,

28. Tappan, *Life of Arthur Tappan*, 232–33.
29. Lesick, *Lane Rebels*, 130.
30. Students' Request for Dismission, para 1.

especially with no other academic destination in mind. Nonetheless, signing their name on this document signified a conviction of greater magnitude than any chosen course of study; in doing so, each student had written their name into history.

The first to sign the document was Huntington Lyman. Nearly fifty years later, Lyman would pen his recollection of the students' historic decision. Lyman recalled, "Those who took the step, long ago, adhere to the decision made. For myself, I cannot see how we could have done differently in consistency with public duty or self-respect."[31] Lyman would eventually be ordained for ministry in Elyria, Ohio, and go on to advocate for abolition tirelessly as a lecturer for the American Anti-Slavery Society.

Among the other students to pen their name to formal requests for dismission were William T. Allan, the head of the antislavery society who was targeted for expulsion by the executive committee of the Lane Board of Trustees. Sereno Streeter's name was there as well. Streeter would later become an agent for the National Anti-Slavery Society. Name by name, each a different story, the students signed the document and made clear their intention to walk away from their chosen school, the seminary they had come to know and love.

While each name tells a different story, one name signifies a very divergent path from the others. Twenty-two names down the list on the original document signed by the students on October 15, 1834, is the name of James Bradley. Bradley's signature was another landmark moment in a remarkable life bursting with them. A journey that began by being ripped from his mother's arms in Africa and brought across the Atlantic Ocean to be sold into slavery as a child. It is a journey marked by anguish, sorrow, and pain. Beaten nearly to the point of death on multiple occasions, Bradley endured to pursue the light of knowledge. Just as he had done previously in purchasing his freedom, Bradley worked with an unmatched discipline to study alongside students that had come from every privilege he had not. His witness and wit fueled the fire of his fellow students during the debates and now, as a free

31. Lyman, "Rebels," 69.

man, Bradley willingly chose to walk away from Lane Theological Seminary.

Theodore Weld, who had passionately opened the debates some eight months previous, now independently expressed his desire to be removed from the enrollment at Lane Theological Seminary. Weld wrote, "To the Faculty of Lane Theological Seminary: Gentlemen, I hereby request a regular dismission from the Lane Theological Seminary. Very Respectfully Yours, Theodore D. Weld. Lane Theological Seminary. October 17, 1834."[32] Among the other students who submitted their request independently was Lorenzo D. Butts. In submitting his request, Butts, who would become a minister later in life, wrote of the cause of abolition that now consumed his heart and mind, "a cause which I will ever think it my duty to firmly advocate."[33]

The decision was now final, the letters signed, sealed, and delivered. This group of so-called rebels were now former students of Lane Theological Seminary. The news of the bold action of these seminary students quickly spread across the antebellum West. While their actions were applauded by many near and far, there were also many critics of the rebellious action taken. This group of seminary students, who, from the perspective of some, ought to have been focused on the preparation for ministry, were simply out of line. Opinions of the students' action were especially divided in the burgeoning metropolis of Cincinnati. The convicted action of the students was having a positive impact through the work they were doing. However, the voices of many who had more influence and power fiercely criticized their actions.

Seemingly unfazed by the ongoings at the seminary, the students continued their work in the city, and within the first few weeks following their official departure from Lane, set plans into motion to procure a place to continue their studies. The students moved away from the Walnut Hills campus of the seminary and congregated in the small town of Cumminsville, a few miles away. President Beecher made one final attempt to reconcile the students

---

32. Weld, Request for Dismission, para 1.
33. Butts, Request for Dismission, para 1.

and the Board, but his previous inaction had, in a twist of irony, set far too much action into motion. The students had been monitoring the ongoing conversation about their actions. The time had come for this group of rebels to communicate their side of the story, not only for their own sake, but also for the sake of so many across the country who were caught up in similar debates regarding the slavery question.

Just before Christmas in December of 1834, a few weeks removed from their decision to walk away from Lane Theological Seminary, the rebels fully adopted their new identity and "issued a fiery attack on the action of the authorities at Lane Theological Seminary and a defense of their own actions."[34] The document was incisive and thorough. The prevailing narrative that fueled the criticism of the students often pointed to their youth and naivety, perhaps suggesting an inferiority of reasoning. The defense of the students, however, left no question about their ability to reason or of the deliberate and thoughtful manner in which they had arrived at their conclusion to leave Lane Theological Seminary in protest.

At the core of the students' formal defense was a plea for the right of free discussion in the context of higher education. As Fletcher noted, "The kernel of it is, of course, an apotheosis of the right of free speech in literary institutions."[35] The students also made it very clear to connect these inalienable rights to the slavery question. The students entitled their work "The Statement of Reasons" and focused their efforts on a clear description of the issues at hand and the critical importance of free discussion within higher education.[36] In addition, the students also sought to ground all of their actions in theological conviction. As Lawrence Lesick noted, "Equally important, the rights of free speech and anti-slavery action were built on a theological foundation that was evangelical, and appropriated from Finney."[37]

---

34. Fletcher, *History of Oberlin*, 162.
35. Fletcher, *History of Oberlin*, 162.
36. Students' Statement of Reasons.
37. Lesick, *Lane Rebels*, 135.

At the top of the students' Statement of Reasons, the purpose of the document was clear:

> Statement of the reasons which have induced the Students of Lane Theological Seminary to dissolve their connection with the Institution. Cincinnati, 1834. The undersigned, recently members of Lane Theological Seminary, having withdrawn from that Institution, desire to lay before the Christian public, the considerations which have influenced them; together with the circumstances which have mainly contributed to such a result.[38]

Signed by a total of fifty-one individuals, this shared testimonial from the Lane Theological Seminary students was meant to communicate in full the central issues of concern. In the Statement of Reasons, the students sought to provide a clear and convincing case for abolition. Equally important to the students cause was to demonstrate how they maintained these persuasions on free speech and abolition on account of, not in spite of, of their grounded theological convictions. The conclusions that had led these students to walk away from Lane Theological Seminary were directly connected to their desire to bear witness and embody their Christian faith. The students saw no separation between the two.

---

38. Students' Statement of Reasons, para 1.

Chapter 5

The Statement of Reasons

A SPIRIT OF FREE INQUIRY

The students' Statement of Reasons opened with background information on just how this unique cohort of students had come to be together at Lane Theological Seminary. There was a serendipitous sense among the students due to an exceptional set of circumstances that led to this unlikely gathering at Lane Theological Seminary in Cincinnati. Some of the students had been among the very first to receive instruction at the seminary when it had opened and many had joined shortly thereafter when the first theological class was established in the fall of 1833. The students had gathered at Lane with a common call, a shared objective at the center of their zeal, namely, the spiritual interests of the West. Set apart for this special work, they came to Lane Theological Seminary in order to go out to the whole world to preach the good news discovered in the gospel of Jesus Christ. The Statement of Reasons described a place to focus their efforts, this area of the country they called the Valley:

> The Valley was our expected field; we assembled here, that we might the more accurately learn its character,

catch the spirit of the gigantic enterprise, grow up into its genius, appreciate its peculiar wants, and be thus qualified by practical skill, no less than by theological erudition, to wield the weapons of truth.[1]

This was not a call that was taken lightly. The students recognized that those who had provided the way for the doors of Lane Theological Seminary to open at Walnut Hills had the highest of expectations that the students might represent the seminary and the church through excellence in both scholarship and practice. As some of the very first to be admitted to the young seminary in Cincinnati, it was a weighty matter to establish an example for all future seminarians at Lane Theological Seminary. They described their collective fervor to "breathe a spirit which might well inspire them; and to leave behind us mantles which they might fitly wear."[2] The students' aim in all of this was to leave Lane Theological Seminary better than when they first arrived, establishing a high moral ground at the seminary for years to come.

If these lofty aims were to be met, the students surmised, they would only be reached by beginning construction upon the firm foundation of free discussion. It is at this point in their statement that they began to lay out what served as an operational thesis, not only for this document, but for all of their actions taken throughout the entirety of the events in question: Free discussion, specifically in the context of higher education, is the duty and inalienable right of all students. Once the necessity for free discussion had been clearly established, the students proceeded to describe in detail a learning progression that had served as a formative process in their education at Lane Theological Seminary; it was an education that began with dialogue, encouraged reflection on duty, and resulted in timely action.

Having established the process of their education, the Statement of Reasons offered some salient examples. The list of examples began with the matter of missions, at home and abroad. In describing their education on missions, the students noted that

1. Students' Statement of Reasons, para 3.
2. Students' Statement of Reasons, para 5.

The Statement of Reasons

they applied the principle of free discussion to missions, and after reflection on their duty, they "acted immediately through liberal contributions."[3] Next, the letter described the students' learning related to temperance, where they found that their duty was clear and they took corresponding action. Another example cited is one of moral reform, where the Statement of Reasons described a process by which the Lane students "examined it in a series of adjourned meetings; light was elicited, principles were fixed, action followed."[4] In each of these matters, the students' process of education followed a similar pattern involving a free discussion of the issue of concern, personal reflection upon their responsibility, and appropriate action determined and taken. Now, having established this pattern throughout their learnings at the seminary, they had come to the question of slavery.

> With the same spirit of free inquiry, we discussed the question of slavery. We prayed much, heard facts, weighed arguments, kept our temper, and after the most patient pondering, in which we were sustained by the excitement of sympathy, not of anger, we decided that slavery was a sin, and as such, ought to be immediately renounced. In this case, too, we acted. We organized an anti-slavery society, and published facts, arguments, remonstrances, and appeals.[5]

The artfully articulated statement delineated a clear connection between free discussion and discernable action. In the case of the abolition of slavery, the students described their zeal for immediate action. Here is how they described their work: "We threw ourselves into the neglected mass of colored population in the city of Cincinnati."[6] Among the actions taken, the students helped support teachers and schools, gave lectures, and preached in multiple churches. The students held no regrets for their convicted action in the city. On the contrary, the Lane Rebels mourned "that

3. Students' Statement of Reasons, para 9.
4. Students' Statement of Reasons, para 9.
5. Students' Statement of Reasons, para 10.
6. Students' Statement of Reasons, para 11.

we have done so little, and suffered so little for those who have lost everything in the vortex of our rapacity, and now all manacled, trampled down, and palsied, cannot help themselves."[7]

The direction of the statement then turned to a detailed description of how the actions taken by the trustees at Lane Theological Seminary were destructive to the idea of free discussion. Free discussion, in the minds of the young seminarians ought to always prevail in the context of higher education. In stark contrast, the actions taken by the seminary's administration—in the view of the students—bore more of resemblance to censorship than to the form of education the students had come to love at Lane. Thus, the decision by the students to leave was rooted first and foremost in the prohibitive actions taken against their free discussion. The Statement of Reasons detailed this idea in full: "The ground of our secession from the seminary is that free discussion and correspondent action have been prohibited by law."[8] The very form of education that had brought the students to Lane Theological Seminary in the first place was now, in their estimation, being outlawed from practice. In essence, the students were no longer being taught how to think, rather, they were being told what to think—a critical distinction in the education of a free and democratic society.

Accordingly, they gave a name to their experience: censorship. The Statement of Reasons recorded their sentiment: "A committee of the board of trustees is set over us to exercise censorship, and vested with discretionary power to dismiss any student whenever they may deem it necessary so to do."[9] Having examined the question of slavery through free discussion, the students sustained a very clear sense of duty in response to their inquiry. Ultimately, it was duty to the cause of Christ, which superseded any previous duty to the seminary and resulted with the secession.

> It is inquiry after immutable truth, whether embodied in the word, or hid in the works of God, or branching out through the relations and duties of man. We bound to

7. Students' Statement of Reasons, para 12.
8. Students' Statement of Reasons, para 13.
9. Students' Statement of Reasons, para 13.

The Statement of Reasons

conduct this search, wherever it may lead, and to adopt the conclusions to which it may bring us. And, whereas, the single object of ascertaining truth is to learn how to act, we are bound to do at once whatever truth dictates to be done.[10]

AN INALIENABLE RIGHT

The Statement of Reasons was structured with a clearly delineated hierarchy of fidelity to which the students felt accountable. While the students' love and regard for Lane Theological Seminary was abundantly clear, their collective statement leaves no question on the matter of final authority; the educational process of discussion and action, after all, from the students' perspective is not conferred by human authority. Accordingly, the authority to take away the right to free discussion ought never to belong in the hands of any human or human institution. The students' Statement of Reasons makes a clear emphasis on delineating this point in full:

> Free discussion being a duty, is consequently a right, and as such, is inherent and inalienable. It is our right. It was before we entered Lane Theological Seminary: privileges we might and did relinquish; advantages might and did receive. But this right the institution "could neither give nor take away." Theological Institutions must of course recognize this immutable principle. Proscription of free discussion is sacrilege! It is boring out the eyes of the soul. It is the robbery of mind. It is the burial of truth. If institutions cannot stand upon this broad footing, let them fall. Better, infinitely better, that the mob demolish every building or the incendiary wrap them in flames; and the young men be sent home to ask their fathers "what is truth?"[11]

If free discussion is the foundation of higher learning, the question of the faculty's role in facilitating such discussion

---

10. Students' Statement of Reasons, para 15.
11. Students' Statement of Reasons, para 15.

naturally comes into focus. The Statement of Reasons composed by the students made it clear that they could never question the authority of their teachers; rather, they viewed their faculty as those who would inform them of their duty to engage in free discussion and to invite them into dialogue that would prompt them to move toward reflection and action. Moreover, it is the duty of faculty to "direct the inquiries of their students; but they must have a care to direct them wholly by principle . . . to inspire them with fresh courage and impel them forward."[12] The faculty hold great power in enabling the powerful change agent of free discussion with the students entrusted to their care. If faculty would choose to deter free discussion to protect either their own interests or the interests of an institution, they would be obstructing the very path of education they sought to clear for students. The students' statement captured this sentiment by describing the inhibition of free discussion as ruin, never remedy.

To their collective dismay, however, the students found more evidence for ruin than remedy in their experience at Lane. They described this in detail. "We looked in vain for that profound veneration for free inquiry . . . Discussion was recognized rather as a privilege which could be granted at the discretion of the faculty, than as a duty and a right above their bestowment."[13] The students had established that they did not hold ill will toward their faculty; however, their joint statement is filled with evidence of disappointment. The students describe what they termed a prominent defect, "that the exciting nature of any question is good ground for forbidding its discussion, and that the unpopularity of moral action warrants its total discontinuance."[14] At the heart of the students' disappointment with their faculty was the evident decision to acquiesce to public sentiment as opposed to engaging in the practice of free discussion that might lead to convicted action. Such a practice of deferring to the prevailing public opinion on matters of great significance was described by the students as wickedness.

12. Students' Statement of Reasons, para 16.
13. Students' Statement of Reasons, para 18.
14. Students' Statement of Reasons, para 19.

What are our theological seminaries to be awed into silence upon the great questions of human duty? Are they to be bribed over to the interests of an unholy public sentiment by promises of patronage or threats of its withdrawal? Shall they be tutored into passivity and thrown to float like dead matter in the wake of the popular will, the satellite and the slave of its shifting vagaries? Are theological students to be put under a board of conservators, with special instructions to stifle all discussion, except on the popular side? In selecting topics for discussion, are the students to avoid those which of great public concernment, whose issues involve all human interest, and whose claims are as wide and deep, as right and wrong and weal and woe can make them? In taking sides upon such questions, the student must needs inquire not where is right and what is duty, not which side is worthy of support, not what will quicken the church, turn the nations from their idols, pioneer into being the glories of the millennium, and cause earth to bloom with the hues of heaven. Ah! Such interrogatories are all out of place. The only questions becoming theological students are, which side are the question popular: which will be huzza'd and hosanna'd? Which will tickle the multitude and soak a sop for the Cerberus of popular favor?[15]

THE EXIGENCIES OF THE AGE

Here the decisive case is made that in contrast to the choice of acquiescing to popular opinion on a contentious matter, the institution of higher education is precisely the place where students should be investigating and discussing the most important, even the most complicated, issues of the age. In preparing themselves for a life of ministry, wherever that might lead, these so-called rebels were convinced of the critical importance of being trained to examine controversial issues in the light of biblical truth and determine an appropriate response. Such a sentiment is articulated in the Statement of Reasons: "Theological students, in determining

15. Students' Statement of Reasons, para 23.

duty, are not to regard the obstacles which grow out of a hostile public sentiment. But how shall duty be determined? We answer by investigation and discussion."[16] The Lane Rebels would not veer far from their understanding of how to approach any issue that may be facing the church or society. They continually return to a clear process that always begins with free discussion as a matter of investigation, moves to reflection to determine duty, and results in fitting action.

The students flatly rejected the premise of the trustees that participation in such a process as it relates to the question of slavery is a distraction or diversion from the more appropriate theological course of studies. In fact, the Statement of Reasons offered a counterargument that an investment in such a process actually serves to accelerate their learning. The students were convinced that the infusion of human emotion with logical thought is a powerful combination in discerning some of the most difficult issues of the age. Of the many issues facing the church and a burgeoning American society in the antebellum period, none rivaled that of the question of slavery. The students saw the issue of slavery and its abolition as the critical question of their day and any course of theological study that did not address a society's most pressing concern seemed hollow at best.

> A subject so deeply freighted with human interests as that of slavery cannot be investigated and discussed intelligently and thoroughly without amplifying and expanding the intellect and increasing the power of its action upon all subjects. Let our institutions engage in discussing subjects of great practical moment; such as slavery, temperance, and moral reform; let them address themselves to the effort, let it be persevered in through an entire course, and they will introduce a new era in mind.[17]

The need to engage and not disregard matters of human interest seemed to be the very crux of the Rebels' decision to walk

---

16. Students' Statement of Reasons, para 24.
17. Students' Statement of Reasons, para 24.

The Statement of Reasons

away from Lane Theological Seminary. If they were being trained to minister in the nineteenth century but could not discuss the most demanding issues contained therein, the training they received is, in the final analysis, woefully inept. Again, the joint defense of the students directly addressed correspondence from the trustees, which had reprimanded them to return their focus to rightly divide the word of truth. The students' Statement of Reasons retorted, "Is a man prepared to 'rightly divide the word of truth, giving to each his portion in due season' who is ignorant of prevailing sins and evils, the moral movements of the day, the spirit of the age?"[18] For these young seminarians, it seemed, a theological education without rightfully acknowledging the spirit of the age was no education at all.

> In short, our theological seminaries will only mock the exigencies of the age, and the expectations of the church, unless they hold their students in contact with these exigencies, that when they have finished their preparation, and are thrown into the midst of them, they may know where they are, and feel at home.[19]

If the argument of the Lane Theological Seminary Board of Trustees was to be boiled down to one primary thought, it was the matter of distraction. Put simply, the trustees held to the belief that the students' engagement with the question of slavery would have been better to be left alone and their focus rightly directed toward the time-tested theological course designated for them since admission. The students fervently disagreed with this line of reasoning; they viewed the trustees' recommendation to focus their energies only on the prescribed course of study to be an admonishment to stand down as it pertains to issues of the day. Through their own investigation of the matter over the course of those eighteen February nights, the students were convinced that inaction was no longer an option afforded them. The students argued, "If he would be guiltless of blood, he must do his utmost to

---

18. Students' Statement of Reasons, para 25.
19. Students' Statement of Reasons, para 25.

unite against it the suffrages of the world. A moral agent cannot determine duty by proxy. He must investigate for himself."[20]

Captured in the students' collective defense were definitions that more clearly articulated what they meant to communicate through some of their chosen terminology. Salient among these definitions is the clarity offered in further delineating the idea upon which the document is based, namely, free discussion. The students defined free discussion as "conversation regulated by rules for the purpose of facilitating an interchange and comparison of sentiments."[21] This operational definition of free discussion offers important clarity toward an understanding of the form of dialogue that can serve a liberating purpose for those involved in any form of protest.

In clearly delineating their rights, the students again offered clarity in defining the form of free discussion—or dialogue—that they believed was most effective for their training.

> Every man has the right freely to investigate every subject submitted to his consideration. He has the same right to conduct this investigation in concert with others; provided it be done at such time and place as not to encroach upon the rights of others. We believe that these rights are not derived from man, that they are inseparable from accountable agency, and inalienable, and, of course, are neither surrendered nor forfeited by membership in theological seminary. Furthermore, we believe, that to prohibit theological students peaceably assembling for the examination of great moral questions, in hours unappropriated to other duties, is an open violation of their rights.[22]

The remit from the trustees had established a rule that any meetings the students held must have a clear and convincing connection to the approved course of study at Lane Theological Seminary. Therefore, it was the stated position of the board that

20. Students' Statement of Reasons, para 26.
21. Students' Statement of Reasons, para 28.
22. Students' Statement of Reasons, para 28.

The Statement of Reasons

no associations or societies ought to be allowed unless that same connection to prescribed studies could be clearly demonstrated. The organization of such societies or assemblies from the perspective of the trustees only serves to distract students' attention and impede their much needed development, and even more so if the topics are matter of public interest or so-called popular excitement.

In direct response, the defense offered by the seminarians challenged the value of an education that did not include free discussion. The students mockingly countered, "Take away the right of assembling, and of speaking when assembled, and he who, from the materials left, can construct free discussion, must be blessed with uncommon invention."[23] Next, the focus of the students' statement turned to apply the vital need for free discussion especially related to the specific matter of slavery—a matter that had been specifically targeted by the board's communication. Anything related to the issue of slavery was declared to have no place at all within the confines of the seminary; thus, an anti-slavery society had no grounds to continue.

From the view of the students, the intentions and purposes of the society were obnoxious in the eyes of the trustees. In fact, the sub-committee of the trustees had not minced words in their shared statement. It was abundantly clear that the board sought to remove any discussion of any kind related to the matter of slavery from the seminary that was entrusted to their care. Even if the faculty had deemed it a topic worthy of discussion in the classroom, it was evident to the students that there was no room for further dialogue on the issue. The students sought clarity on this perplexing matter.

> Now, we ask, will the faculty of Lane Theological Seminary permit the subject of slavery to be discussed in the Institution, when the board of trustees formally declare their conviction that it ought to be excluded? To expect such permission from them, before discussions upon

---

23. Students' Statement of Reasons, para 37.

slavery become popular with the community, argues either ignorance of facts, or insensibility to evidence.[24]

UNCHECKED POWER

While the students were clearly irritated by the first order in the trustees' communication, it was the second order that had truly caused tensions to rise. The second order equipped the executive committee with what the students deemed extraordinary, unchecked power to outright dismiss any student from Lane Theological Seminary when they shall think it necessary to do so. This is an important distinction in the growing chasm between the students and trustees of Lane Theological Seminary. The board was no longer referring to matters of education and curriculum, but of absolute, and apparently unrestrained, power.

From the perspective of the students, this simply did not stand the test of just action. They argued that the executive committee had unilaterally been granted the power to "dismiss any student when they think it necessary to do so! No opportunity afforded the student to rebut charges, confront witnesses, meet an accuser face-to-face, plead a justification, or prove an alibi."[25] In a sharp rebuke, the Statement of Reasons offered by the students appealed, "Let history testify to its practical operations, and be the commentator upon its spirit. As soon as the board had clothed the executive committee with this extraordinary power, a meeting was immediately to exercise it."[26] The exercise of the power the students now referred to were the resolutions to dismiss several key members among them. To make their intentions crystal clear the Executive Committee promptly dismissed Professor John Morgan of the academic department of the seminary. They also considered the expulsion of two students, Theodore Weld and William T. Allan, the latter the president of the anti-slavery society. The students

---

24. Students' Statement of Reasons, para 39.
25. Students' Statement of Reasons, para 40.
26. SStudents' Statement of Reasons, para 41.

The Statement of Reasons

sought to explain their deep concern by depicting the gravity of such action: "To be dismissed from a theological seminary for a sufficient cause is a stigma not easily effaced; and the sufficiency of the cause is always supposed, unless the contrary be shown."[27] In levying a devastating blow to the seminary, the Statement of Reasons positioned the institution in the same company of other historical parties who had wielded reckless power.

> The Pope excommunicates only when "he thinks it necessary so to do." The inquisition order to the rack only "when they think it necessary so to do." The Divan consigned to the bastinado and the bowstring only "when they think it necessary so to do." The Star Chamber and the Council of Ten tortured, banished, and brought to the block, only "when they thought it necessary so to do." Eighteen hundred thirty-four has nominated a new candidate for the catalogue, and added another star to the constellation. The executive committee of Lane Theological Seminary thrust from the Institution "any student when they think it necessary so to do."[28]

At times, the Statement of Reasons operated as more of an exposé, intended to share with the wider public elements of the story that were not regularly being reported by other media outlets. The seminarians were left with no doubt it was the intention of the board to repress and reject their right to free discussion. The board had declared that they saw no danger of too much restraint and that they fully intended to equip faculty with all authority to wield influence over the conduct of the students. The students' Statement of Reasons exposed to a national audience an all-too-compelling story that President Beecher and the board longed to keep concealed. "We do not wonder that the president of the board begged as he did, that this extraordinary order might not be published to the world."[29] The students overtly expressed that the trustees' doctrine prohibiting the formation of associations or

---

27. Students' Statement of Reasons, para 41.
28. Students' Statement of Reasons, para 41.
29. Students' Statement of Reasons, para 43.

societies was a policy to which they could not, in good conscience, subscribe to. Doing so would violate their understanding of free discussion as an inalienable right to all regardless of the institution of which one belongs.

The students delineated two essential reasons why they could not comply. First, compliance would be the effective surrender of the inalienable right to free discussion. Second, the purpose for the anti-slavery society was a commitment to operate against the system of slavery and its allies. Thus, until those have been abolished and defeated, the members of the society must forbid its dissolution. In the reinforcement of their resolve, the students offered a passionate plea:

> Is this a time to lay hands upon our mouths, when the ambassadors of Christ hold as merchandise, and sell for filthy lucre, the members of his own body; and with the price of blood in their hands, still break the sacramental bread? When the shepherds of God's flock instead of carrying his lambs in their arms, tear them from the fold, and hurl them to be rent by wolves—and yet are caressed by the church, accounted faithful shepherds and worthy of all honor? No!—with heart, and soul, and mind, and strength, we answer, No! We cannot betray inviolable trusts; we cannot break our plighted faith; we cannot surrender inalienable rights; we will not shout hosanna in the train of arbitrary power, not plot treason against humanity, nor apostatize from God. No! God forbid that we should abandon a cause that strikes its roots so deep into the soil of human interests, and human rights, and throws its branches upward and abroad, so high and wide, into the sunlight of human hopes, and human well-being.[30]

One of the reasons provided by the board for the seminarians to abstain from the slavery debate was the idea that the seminary is not meant to be the arbiter of questions upon which Christians differ in their thinking. In response, the Statement of Reasons offered numerous examples of issues on which Christians disagree.

---

30. Students' Statement of Reasons, para 45.

The Statement of Reasons

Among the examples provided are missions, the dissemination of the Bible, the importance of camp meetings, and the long-lived debate over whether a sermon should be read from a written manuscript or presented in an extemporaneous manner. The students made the case that if the seminary is to be filled with students who do not take sides or express opinions that Lane Theological Seminary administration will have to face immense difficulty in filling its classrooms. The students rhetorically asked where the institution might find "a sufficient quantity of neutrals, non-commitals, non-descripts, and nullities for such an emergency? Such commodities are not on sale in the western market, and we know the East too well to recommend importation from that quarter."[31]

The defense of the students tactically approached each and every declaration issued by the board and brought them under the light of scrutiny. They sought to examine the charges sanctimoniously levied by the trustees through a review of the methods used to obtain the information on which they had been based. While the board had described a process by which they reviewed all matters pertaining to the issue and collected the necessary information, the students were never consulted. The board had not displayed hitherto a propensity either to hear the students' perspective on what had transpired at Lane Theological Seminary thus far or to seek out the motives and intentions that had inspired the institution of the anti-slavery society.

In their shared Statement of Reasons the students described no evidence of effort "on the part of the trustees, who aided in the passage of those rules and orders, an almost total nonintercourse with all the students except those whose views were similar to their own."[32] Rather, the weighty decisions of the trustees had been arrived at, from the perspective of the seminarians, through vague rumors and false reports. Even though one of the charges had been focused on the students' apparent neglect of study, none of the board had been present at the exams in the previous term. The students pointed to this as an example of a "favorable opportunity

---

31. Students' Statement of Reasons, para 49.
32. Students' Statement of Reasons, para 54.

to have acquired specific information on that point, inasmuch as the examination continued a week, and two-thirds of the trustees and all the executive committee reside but two miles from the seminary."[33]

As for the trustees who had interacted with the ostensible rebels, only three of the twenty-five board members had intimate knowledge of the students and their society; these also happened to be the only members that had voted *against* the orders. The board had detailed a disproportionate interest on the part of the students in the issue of slavery, but there was no evidence in the students' academic engagement. Not only had they continued in their course of study, many among their number had repeatedly turned down invitations to deliver public addresses on the subject of slavery.

In addition, the defense offered a detailed and nuanced response to the notion that the seminary had been in a state of anarchy or that there had been some form of open war between the students and faculty there. The students cited a sermon that had been preached by Professor Calvin Stowe in which he "expressly declared all such representations as totally false. He vindicated the character of the students, asserted their diligence in study, their respectful demeanor towards the faculty, their obedience to law, and their Christian deportment."[34] The Statement of Reasons left nothing to question as the students boldly asserted that every law and request of the seminary "has been implicitly obeyed by us, and that the utmost harmony has existed between the students and the faculty. Difference of opinion upon the subject of slavery has never interfered with the reciprocal interchange of courtesy and affection."[35]

The Board of Trustees had also laid the burden of the seminary's now uncertain future on the decision made by the students to leave. In similar fashion to the previous arguments, the students refuted the assertion of the board with remarkable data. The

---

33. Students' Statement of Reasons, para 54.
34. Students' Statement of Reasons, para 61.
35. Students' Statement of Reasons, para 62.

The Statement of Reasons

students noted that they, in fact, had the names of forty students who were intending to continue in the theological department who had "signified their intention after the results of our discussion on the subject of slavery were fully known to the public, and before the executive committee had published their report."[36]

Moreover, the Statement of Reasons described more than forty students who were intending to enter the literary department. The students also described the experiences of the aforementioned theological students of which twenty-four had been deterred from entering. According to the students, the literary department had experienced a similar devastation due to the conduct of the trustees. The students' Statement of Reasons made a clear and convincing argument that the "present dilapidated condition of the seminary is not in consequence of 'the proceedings among the students on the subject of slavery'; but has been caused by 'the decisive measures' of the trustees."[37]

The report of the trustees had also delegitimized the organization of the anti-slavery society, noting that it had been assembled without appropriate consent. The students responded to this by offering a reminder that not only had it received proper consent, the preamble and constitution of the anti-slavery society were read to President Beecher himself, prior to being published. The students' statement made note that the entire spirit of their society had received the blessing and sanction of the President.

The collective defense of the students proceeded to offer substantial detail related to rumors surrounding their purported behavior in going about the work of the anti-slavery society in Cincinnati. Many of the fanatical anecdotes sought to bring into question the motives of the students in their work throughout the city. The students made it clear that while they have belabored their points in detail they did so to ensure that all of the facts were openly presented. In their joint statement the students wanted to ensure that they clearly and transparently distanced themselves from the evils of racism. They abhorred the behavior of those who

---

36. Students' Statement of Reasons, para 67.
37. Students' Statement of Reasons, para 69.

"would either blush with shame or redden with rage, to sit at the same table, kneel at the same altar, occupy the same seat at church, or board in the same family, with worth, respectability, and virtue, 'if guilty of a skin not colored like its own.'"[38]

The diagnosis of the evil of racism established with precise clarity the separating point between the students and the trustees. While the trustees and other leaders, who held closely to the central tenets of the American Colonization Society, might have blushed to share a table with a person of color, the students had revealed a different way, a better way. In stark contrast, the students demonstrated the values of family, worth, respectability, and virtue in the communion they sensed with fellow student, James Bradley. The kind of respect and honor the students sought to express through the anti-slavery society across the city of Cincinnati had been underway in their midst right there on the Walnut Hills campus of the Lane Theological Seminary.

JAMES BRADLEY

James Bradley's awe-inspiring testimony through the free discussion afforded at the debates played a critical role in turning the tide among the Lane Theological Seminary students. As the students concluded their defense, Bradley once again was a character of great magnitude in the story of the Lane Rebels. The students' Statement of Reasons detailed an important story involving Bradley that illustrated that the kind of worth and value they sought to work toward—worth and value that had been exemplified by none other than President Beecher:

> While upon this point, we take pleasure in stating a fact, highly honorable to the president of Lane Theological Seminary. At the close of the last term, Dr. Beecher invited the students of the Seminary to take tea with him, together with the professors and their families, and some gentlemen from the city. When the company were assembled, the Dr. expressed his regret to some

---

38. Students' Statement of Reasons, para 78.

The Statement of Reasons

of us and has frequently done it since, that our colored brother, James Bradley, was not present; and said, if he had dreamed of his being absent, he would have gone himself and insisted upon his coming.

It may not be known to all, that this brother is a native of AFRICA; was stolen in childhood, and sold into slavery, in South Carolina. A year and a half ago, he purchased his own body, and joined this Institution. He now leaves it, unwilling to surrender, again, inalienable rights, or to aid in the destruction of a society of which he is a beloved member, and officer, and which he assisted in organizing, for the redemption of his poor perishing brethren.[39]

The story of James Bradley was a fitting conclusion to the Statement of Reasons composed by the students ten days before Christmas, December 15, 1834. Bradley's improbable journey from the shores of West Africa to a childhood spent in slavery, to the campus of Lane Theological Seminary, is emblematic of the kind of transformation that had become now so readily apparent in their midst. Bradley, nearly beaten to death on more than one occasion, worked through countless sleepless nights to purchase his freedom and pursue the light of knowledge. His arrival at Lane Theological Seminary to join a student body that also included Theodore Weld, James Thome, Huntington Lyman, and other like-minded students seemed serendipitous if not ordained.

While some of the students had knowledge that fueled their abolitionist ambition, none had felt the blow of a currycomb to their head; none had endured a multitude of sleepless nights wondering if their life would end the next day. Bradley's desire for education at the seminary and his gracious disposition toward all despite the pain he had withstood shone a light so brightly none who gathered for the famed debates at Lane Theological Seminary would ever look at the question of slavery the same.

After referencing Bradley, the Statement of Reasons concluded with one final delineation of the facts that ultimately led to their signatures on a joint letter of dismission. The students

39. Students' Statement of Reasons, paras 78–79.

concluded with a clear declaration that the withdrawal from their beloved school was not due to the exercise of supervision on the part of the trustees and faculty. Their supervision over the students was a right they affably accepted. Further, the students' decision to withdraw was not over differences in ideology as it pertained to the question of slavery, nor was it in response to the academic experience they had at Lane Theological Seminary, of which they were clearly grateful or in response to any shame related to the actions they had taken through the anti-slavery society. While the aforementioned issues may have caused consternation, none of the above concerns, individually or in aggregate, was enough to push the students away from their studies at Lane Theological Seminary. No, the students' withdrawal was very simply a statement on the critical importance of the right to free discussion.

> But we leave, because the authorities above us have asserted the right to suspend free discussion upon their own arbitrary wills. Because they sanction the principle of prostration to public sentiment, corrupt and desperate as it is, by avowing the doctrine that discussion must be directed according to popular will . . . Because they will allow us no alternative but abandoning the cause of universal liberty and love, or withdrawing from Lane Theological Seminary.[40]

The students' affection for the people and purpose that held together this little seminary at Walnut Hills was evident to the end. However, the cause of abolition had taken up residence in their hearts. They were deeply convicted and zealously committed to the work of abolition, as an appropriate response to what they believed was the revealed truth from God—that all men are created equal. Their statement made it clear that their love for Lane Theological Seminary was strong, but as the students noted, "the great principles for which we contend are dearer far."[41] There was no amount of compromise, selfish prospect, or favor that would divert them from this work in which they now felt implicated.

---

40. Students' Statement of Reasons, para 81.
41. Students' Statement of Reasons, para 82.

The Statement of Reasons

Despite the rebellious label they had been given, the Statement of Reasons clearly communicated the students' shared regard for Lane Theological Seminary, "We leave Lane Theological Seminary with sentiments of grateful affection for the advantages which, during our membership, it so largely afforded us."[42] Perhaps due to that depth of love felt by the students, they also mourned its condition. They described their deep sorrow that in crushing free discussion, "its ruling authorities have given a death blow to the spirit of its glory, and have dragged it down to a dishonored level with those institutions where mind becomes the crouching slave of prescription."[43] Having expressed their sorrow, the students delivered a parting blow to the seminary by putting its leadership in the company of those "where siding with the strong against the weak, with the doers against the sufferers of wrong, is the stipulated condition of membership."[44]

The final proclamation in the exhaustive defense of the students' withdraw from Lane Theological Seminary offered what may be viewed as a manifesto for what the students once believed distinguished the work of the seminary. From their perspective, the seminary existed for the very purpose of preparing students who "need, above all things, in an age such as this, the pure and impartial, the disinterested and magnanimous, the uncompromising and fearless, in combination with the gentle and tender spirit and example of Christ."[45] Even in their departure from Lane Theological Seminary, the students held out hope that it may someday be again restored to the glory of its beginning.

Once completed, the Statement of Reasons was signed by fifty-one former students of Lane Theological Seminary. Among the students to sign were James Bradley, Theodore Weld, William T. Allan, Huntington Lyman, James Thome, and Sereno Streeter. At the bottom of the document a postscript noted that there were several others who agreed with what was written in the statement

42. Students' Statement of Reasons, para 83.
43. Students' Statement of Reasons, para 83.
44. Students' Statement of Reasons, para 83.
45. Students' Statement of Reasons, para 84.

but were several hundred miles away from the seminary and unable to sign it themselves. The students noted that their defense had been prepared five weeks earlier, but they delayed its publication at the request of certain individuals. Historian Lawrence T. Lesick noted, "By November 10, it was nearly completed, but was later withheld from publication, apparently at the faculty's request. After much anticipation, the Statement of Reasons appeared in early January 1835."[46]

CRITICAL RECEPTION

The critical reception of the media varied. The local papers in Cincinnati "generally approved the actions of the faculty and trustees."[47] In contrast, the *Catholic Telegraph* in Cincinnati was "the only local paper to criticize openly (and satirically) the trustees and faculty."[48] The news of the students' withdrawal reached across the country, where the debate on the question of slavery raged on. Multiple papers supported the students. *The Liberator* "responded to the passage of the laws by calling Lane Theological Seminary 'a Bastille of Oppression—a Spiritual Inquisition.'"[49] However, numerous media outlets clearly supported the side of the trustees, noting that this was an issue of control, not abolition.

Among those to speak in favor of the students' action was Joshua Leavitt, editor of the *New York Evangelist*. The *New York Evangelist* had a wide readership, especially among those who sought the abolition of slavery, and would later play an important role in securing an educational home for the Lane Rebels. Leavitt's charges against the leadership were rooted in the persuasion that the restrictions and executive orders actually had very little to do with institutional control. Instead, argued Leavitt, the real reason

---

46. Lesick, *Lane Rebels*, 135.
47. Lesick, *Lane Rebels*, 142.
48. Lesick, *Lane Rebels*, 142.
49. Lesick, *Lane Rebels*, 143.

The Statement of Reasons

could be summarized as simply wanting to stop the students' equal treatment of Blacks.

In addition to Leavitt's support, some of the major donors that provided the means to establish the seminary were disappointed in the actions taken by the trustees and expressed their discontentment with the direction of the seminary. Arthur Tappan would continue to pay President Beecher's salary until 1837, but he clearly expressed that he was disappointed in the actions of the Lane Board of Trustees. The students' withdrawal from Lane Theological Seminary drew attention to what was becoming a regular occurrence on the campuses of higher education across antebellum America. "The conflicts concerning the relationship between students and faculty and over the role of education in society demonstrated the extent to which slavery had insinuated itself into the major institutions of American society."[50] While similar debates carried on across the country, the "Seminary's location on the border of a slave state, its talented student body, and its nationally known president provided a dramatic setting and cast."[51] The story of the action taken by the Lane Theological Seminary students emboldened abolitionist activity wherever it was told.

---

50. Lesick, *Lane Rebels*, 145.
51. Lesick, *Lane Rebels*, 146.

Chapter 6

Rebels with a Cause

The Lane Theological Seminary students were rebels with a cause but no longer a campus. Meanwhile, in the early autumn of 1834, Oberlin College was more like a campus without much of a cause; the school was without a president and lacked professors. It was during this time that Reverend John Keep was tapped to serve as the chair of the Board of Trustees. Reverend Keep was a renowned advocate for female education and a decided friend of the abolitionist movement; Keep had previously founded a free school for Black students to pursue their education.

Co-founder of Oberlin College Reverend John Jay Shipherd was an avid reader of the aforementioned *New York Evangelist*, which had covered the proceedings at Lane Theological Seminary in detail. In the aftermath of what had transpired at Lane, Shipherd saw a unique opportunity to bring new life to Oberlin College—a place where the students' cause would be gladly embraced—a measure that could result in a stabilizing effect to the fledgling college. Shipherd acted quickly; he went on to his fateful destination by settling into the back of an uncomfortable mail wagon, his quiet co-sojourners the bags of letters and papers that surrounded him.

Shipherd planned to meet with Reverend Asa Mahan and the Lane Theological Seminary Rebels. The students had already indicated they were favorable to the idea of coming to Oberlin College, but only if the following conditions were met: Asa Mahan as the new president, John Morgan a member of the faculty, and Charles Finney to teach theology. In addition to these matters of personnel, the students resolved to demand the guarantee of freedom of speech on all reform issues, and lastly, while certainly not the least in magnitude: an official policy that ensured that Black students would be admitted in the same manner as White students.

A SEMINARY OF OUR OWN

The days immediately following the students' exodus from Lane Theological Seminary were filled with the joy and energy discovered in the zealous work of abolition. Even as the students walked away from the seminary at Walnut Hills, they had little idea of where to go next. Huntington Lyman described the days immediately following: "We went out, not knowing wither we went. The Lord's hand was with us."[1] A core group of the Rebels found a temporary home not far from the Lane campus. Five miles from the seminary, the students discovered a deserted brick tavern, "with many convenient rooms. Here we rallied. A gentleman of the vicinity offered us all necessary fuel, a gentleman far off sent us a thousand dollars, and we set up a seminary of our own."[2]

With the newly formed school of sorts in nearby Cumminsville, the students went about their work of abolition in the city of Cincinnati. As a matter of first priority, the students immediately chartered a new anti-slavery society. "The chief officers of the society were given to the young men from south of the river in order to give special prominence to their participation: Allan was president; Robinson, vice-president; even James Bradley was listed among the 'Managers.'"[3] In addition to the seminarians, there were women who joined the rebels in their work, "The

1. Lyman, "Rebels," 66.
2. Lyman, "Rebels," 66.
3. Fletcher, *History of Oberlin*, 154.

Sisters—Phebe Mathews, Emeline Bishop, Lucy Wright, and Maria Fletcher—continued to cooperate in the teaching."[4]

The students strategically planned their tactics in going about the cause of immediate emancipation. They created a committee to find the addresses of men of influence in all the land to petition to join their cause. In addition, other committees were formed and given a remit to carry forward. One of the committees prepared a document that laid out the doctrine of immediate emancipation and printed a multitude of copies for distribution. Accordingly, "a committee of the whole folded and directed this document and sent it abroad to all the winds." It was a time Lyman described as one of "cyclones and thunderings, and an earthquake. Portents appeared and voices were heard. Tokens were abroad in the earth and waterspouts in the heavens."[5]

The early returns on the students' investment in Cincinnati were fruitful. Theodore Weld reported some of the exciting developments in a letter:

> We have established five day schools among the three thousand colored people of Cincinnati; a Lyceum with tri-weekly lectures; evening schools for teaching adults to read; Sabbath schools and Bible classes. We are also trying to establish a reading-room and library for them. I have never seen such eagerness to acquire knowledge, nor such rapidity of acquisition.[6]

Not all of the students who signed the Statement of Reasons stayed together in Cumminsville. In fact, some students sought to continue their studies at other institutions or chose to return home. There was a core group of the rebels, however, that were committed to communion with one another in their shared work of abolition. The "nucleus of Oneidas and leaders in the anti-slavery work kept together and established at nearby Cumminsville an informal Seminary of their own."[7]

4. Fletcher, *History of Oberlin*, 166.
5. Lyman, "Rebels," 63.
6. Weld, Letter, para 1.
7. Fletcher, *History of Oberlin*, 165.

Lesick summarized it in this way: "Of the seventy-five Lane Rebels, little or nothing is known about twenty-one, other than that they did not return to the seminary in the fall of 1834."[8] After signing their names to the joint letter of dismission in October, the core group continued their work from their makeshift seminary in the deserted brick tavern a few miles away. From the beginning of November 1834, the Lane Rebels "studied their favorite subjects, listened to a few lectures on physiology from Dr. Gamaliel Bailey... and commuted into Cincinnati to continue their benevolent work."[9]

The months of November and December in Ohio can offer some challenging conditions, especially for a group of seminary students who called a deserted brick tavern their home. Nearly fifty years removed from his days in that old abandoned tavern, Huntington Lyman reflected on the paradoxical experience of living in awful conditions while doing such meaningful work. Not only were the living conditions often challenging, the attacks from those who opposed their work were becoming all too familiar. Lyman wrote, "A few months of exciting and dispiriting experience followed, we became familiar with harsh words and the more solid missives—stale eggs, brick bats, and tar."[10]

Even in the face of such adverse conditions and crude human behavior, these Lane Theological Seminary Rebels could not help but to be joyful and encouraged in participating in the work of abolition. Lyman recounted, "But in our despondency this was our cheer: Calhoun, Wise, and Toombs, in Congress, would advance the monstrous assumptions of slavery, and then the devotees of the North, like Buchanan, Cass, Hendricks, and Atherton, would bow down in worship."[11] The tide was starting to turn against the evil of slavery in antebellum America, and these young seminarians were jubilant at the notion that they were a part of something so much bigger than themselves—a movement that was gaining

8. Lesick, *Lane Rebels*, 167.
9. Fletcher, *History of Oberlin*, 165.
10. Lyman, "Rebels," 68.
11. Lyman, "Rebels," 68.

momentum all across their young country. Lyman recalled, "We were humbled, feeling ourselves to be mere symptoms in the great fight; but we were comforted, and could laugh until sleep came on."[12]

Despite their living conditions, making a home out of a deserted tavern in the winter, and in spite of the constant attacks of their opponents, there was an evident joy in the hearts of these students sustained by the deeply rooted belief that they were doing what God had called them to do. Nonetheless, the conditions for their continued work were simply not sustainable. They longed to complete the formal ministry training they had begun at Lane Theological Seminary. "This halcyon life could not well be permanent; it was not indeed quite satisfactory. There was need of haste to complete their theological education. But where should they go?"[13] "Our next step brought us to Oberlin, where a kind hospitality awaited us, which no words can depict."[14]

OBERLIN

The story of Oberlin College begins with the friendship of Reverend John Jay Shipherd and the famed evangelical revivalist Charles Grandison Finney. Shipherd and Finney shared a passion for evangelism and sought to bring about God's kingdom on earth through sharing his word with the masses. Shipherd and Finney joined forces in Rochester, New York, where they temporarily shared the preaching load at Rochester's Second Church. Despite Finney's urging to stay in the east, Shipherd felt compelled to take his evangelistic ministry to the west and embarked on a journey that would conclude in Elyria, Ohio, of Lorain County. It did not take long for Shipherd's fiery preaching to spark a revival among the residents of Elyria and the surrounding communities.

---

12. Lyman, "Rebels," 68.
13. Fletcher, *History of Oberlin*, 166.
14. Lyman, "Rebels," 68.

J. Brent Morris described the story of Oberlin as an "idea before it was a place."[15] The seeds of this idea germinated in the heart and mind of John Jay Shipherd as he plotted with his boyhood friend Philo Pennfield Stewart. Shipherd and Stewart dreamed of a colony that included the institution of a new school that would train both young men and women for the work of the ministry. As their dream began to take shape, the two friends decided to name the colony Oberlin "after the French clergyman John Frederic Oberlin (1740–1826) whose compassionate social work in an isolated area of Alsace for sixty years had earned him worldwide recognition."[16] Shortly after establishing a church in this newly formed colony, Shipherd began the work of establishing the school. "The founders aimed at the education of the 'whole man,' yet women would be welcome as well when the school's doors opened to students December 3, 1833, making Oberlin College the nation's first coeducational collegiate institution."[17]

Shortly thereafter, students, compelled by the institute's mission, arrived in Oberlin to begin their studies only to find that there were not sufficient funds to pay the faculty. At the end of the first academic year at Oberlin College, over one hundred students were enrolled. Students, even after discovering the school was full, would make the long trip to Oberlin anyway, "often hundreds of miles, to beg for admission in person."[18] In October of 1834, the same month that the students at Lane Theological Seminary had signed their exit papers just down the road in Cincinnati, Henry Brown made the decision to resign as president of the Oberlin College Board of Trustees. The Oberlin Collegiate Institute had noble ambition but little in regard to leadership or teaching staff to sustain its mission.

In late 1834, the Reverend John Keep was asked to step into the leadership of the Oberlin College Board of Trustees. Reverend Keep had come to Ohio through a similar path as Shipherd; Keep

15. Morris, *Hotbed of Abolitionism*, 12.
16. Morris, *Hotbed of Abolitionism*, 16.
17. Morris, *Hotbed of Abolitionism*, 17.
18. Morris, *Hotbed of Abolitionism*, 17.

had felt a sense of calling to bring the gospel message to the western territories of America. Father Keep had long been an advocate for female education and had worked tirelessly in the city of Cleveland to advance opportunities for people of color. Having once been an activist for colonization, Keep shifted in his beliefs and began his tenure at Oberlin College convinced that "immediate emancipation without colonization as the proper solution of the evil."[19]

On September 23, 1834, the Oberlin College Board of Trustees held a meeting to discuss the financial challenges crippling the Institute. A decision was made that Shipherd should travel to raise the financial means necessary. In doing so, he would have opportunity to share the Institute's desperate need and perhaps secure the support needed to sustain the Oberlin mission. Shipherd was unaware of "the progress of eastern immediatists or of Finney's departure when he set out from Oberlin College in search of the revivalist's guidance on the mission that many Oberlin Collegeites thought could be the final lifesaving measure for the college."[20]

Shipherd, a regular subscriber to the aforementioned *New York Evangelist*, had been following the series of events that had led to the exodus of students from the Lane Theological Seminary in Cincinnati. His admiration of the principled stance taken by the students at Lane Theological Seminary made Cincinnati a natural choice for his first destination. "The journey to Mansfield over the miry, rutted roads of late autumn he found 'slow and tedious' especially with the 'baulky sullen horse' provided him by one of the Oberlin colonists."[21] Shipherd could not have imagined what would become of his Oberlin dream as he set out on this fateful journey. On November 24, 1834, Shipherd and his horse "limped away from northwestern Ohio, the school's debts were in arrears, it was in desperate need of more sufficient facilities, its board of trustees was deserting, and its first annual report reflected the dismal state of college administration."[22]

19. Fletcher, *History of Oberlin*, 167–68.
20. Morris, *Hotbed of Abolitionism*, 23.
21. Fletcher, *History of Oberlin*, 168.
22. Morris, *Hotbed of Abolitionism*, 23.

Shipherd may have had an expectant sense about the Lane Rebels. They clearly maintained a theological resolve and a philosophical alignment with Oberlin College leadership concerning the abolition of slavery. Shipherd may have learned more through his relationship with John Keep. The younger Keep, Theodore, had planned to begin his studies at Lane Theological Seminary, but due to what had transpired there had made the decision to return home to Oberlin. While traveling to Cincinnati with his self-described "baulky sullen horse," Shipherd met with Theodore Keep in Columbus. Theodore shared confirmation of the "fascinating rumors that Shipherd had heard echoing across the Ohio countryside."[23]

As Shipherd began to gather further information about the purported rebels from Walnut Hills, the former Lane Theological Seminary students continued to congregate in Cumminsville throughout the early winter months of 1835. The students continued their theological studies and their work toward immediate emancipation of all slaves. As the students considered their future, "a rumor had circulated since November that a new theological seminary would be established in the West which would guarantee free speech."[24]

Shipherd forged ahead in his journey, riding in a mail wagon, packed among the bags of letters and papers. The next stop on the journey was Cincinnati and the home of Asa Mahan. Mahan had served on the Lane Theological Seminary Board of Trustees but had parted ways in disagreement with the decision rendered in response to the anti-slavery society formed by the students. In listening to Mahan share of what had transpired at Lane Theological Seminary and hearing of his fervent passion for education and abolition, Shipherd had not only found a kindred spirit but the man who he believed ought to serve as the first president of the Oberlin Collegiate Institute. The students who had exited the seminary trusted Mahan implicitly and had already resolved that Mahan's presence would be a determining factor in any new direction.

23. Morris, *Hotbed of Abolitionism*, 24.
24. Fletcher, *History of Oberlin*, 169.

The Light of Knowledge

Since their move from Walnut Hills, the work of the students at Cumminsville had been sustained thus far through the generosity of a man by the name of Arthur Tappan. Arthur, along with his brother, Lewis, were anti-slavery philanthropists from the East Coast that had financially supported the convicted action of the abolitionist movement at Lane Theological Seminary. Since hearing about the proceedings at the seminary, the Tappans had been urging the evangelist Charles Finney to make the journey west to assume teaching responsibilities for the students in an educational environment where free speech would be a guarantee. Finney would later reflect, "Arthur Tappan's heart was as large as all New York, and I might say as large as the world."[25]

Arthur and Lewis Tappan were "definitely committed to financing them wherever they went."[26] The conditions seemed favorable, if not opportune, to Shipherd; not only could Oberlin College have an influx of mature and serious-minded students, the Institute could also gain a new president in Mahan and excellent teaching faculty in both his friend Charles Finney and the esteemed John Morgan. Shipherd, now accompanied by Mahan, journeyed east to secure a commitment from their friend Finney. Once they arrived in New York and extended the formal invitation, Finney agreed to come to Oberlin College on the same conditions of the students at Cumminsville: the trustees must commit to the protection of free speech and all students, regardless of their race, would be welcome to enroll at Oberlin. If these conditions were met, the funding would be provided by Arthur and Lewis Tappan.

Lewis Tappan wrote a biography depicting the life of his brother, Arthur. Tappan recalled the events leading up to the proposal for the efforts of the Lane Theological Seminary Rebels to merge streams with Shipherd and his colleagues at Oberlin College. Tappan noted,

> A large number of them made arrangements to repair to Oberlin College Seminary, Ohio, having received satisfactory assurances that no attempt would be made to

---

25. Finney, *Autobiography*, 304.
26. Fletcher, *History of Oberlin*, 169.

prevent free discussion, or oppose the resolution of the students to repudiate caste, and treat the colored people, in the seminary and out of it, as equal with themselves before the law and the gospel.[27]

At Oberlin College, one of the first residence halls would be known as Tappan Hall, for which Arthur had contributed twelve thousand dollars to the Institute. In his volume on Arthur, Lewis Tappan recounted a letter from Finney in which he described a reluctance to leave New York but that he was persuaded by Shipherd and Mahan to spend his summers instructing the students at Oberlin College. Tappan recalled that his brother Arthur was deeply moved by the work of abolition. Lewis Tappan wrote of his brother's desire to build up an institution that accepts "colored students upon the same conditions that you do White students; and see that the work not be taken out of the hands of the faculty, and spoiled by the trustees, as was the case at Lane Theological Seminary."[28] The Tappan brothers played in important part in advancing the students' cause. Finney would later recognize Arthur Tappan's vital role: "The fact is that Oberlin turned the scale in all of the Northwest. No man can tell the story right unless he knows this ... [Tappan's] promise was the condition of existence of Oberlin as it has been."[29]

SHIPHERD'S PLEA

Shipherd was now convinced that the shared convictions of the Lane Rebels and those at Oberlin College were meant for union. Convincing the trustees and students at Oberlin College, however, would be an arduous challenge. The Rebels had seen too much at Lane Theological Seminary and had come much too far to agree to join another institution without specific conditions met. "Most importantly, they required that African Americans be admitted to

---

27. Tappan, *Life of Arthur Tappan*, 237–38.
28. Tappan, *Life of Arthur Tappan*, 239–40.
29. Tappan, *Life of Arthur Tappan*, Appendix 8.

Oberlin College together with and on the same terms as White students."[30] Shipherd initiated a resolution to be discussed at the next meeting of the Oberlin College trustees in an effort to fully comply with the Lane Theological Seminary contingency's conditions.

Shipherd's exuberance for this new direction for the Institute was countered by fear and panic from those back in Oberlin. Some of these fears were founded upon the violent blowback experienced at other institutions where such measures had been taken. The trustees at Oberlin worried "that Black admissions would so enrage outsiders that they might converge on the town and destroy the school."[31] Shipherd sought to speak calm into the chaos. On January 27, 1835, Shipherd penned one of two pastoral letters to the brethren and sisters at Oberlin. These letters, sent during his time in New York, were "perhaps the two most important letters in Oberlin College's early history."[32]

In honor of his commitment to the authority of scripture, Shipherd opened the letter in a similar fashion to the Apostle Paul's letter to the Philippians. He reminded the beloved in Oberlin that the one which hath begun a good work would indeed perform it. Shipherd set the tone for his plea: "Trusting that you reciprocate my Christian love and confidence, I speak freely as unto my children, my brethren and my sisters in the Lord."[33] In this confidence, Shipherd challenged his readers that if they would do their duty Oberlin College would be a living fountain and remembered for generations to come.

In the body of his pastoral letter, Shipherd fully expressed the crux of his concern. Being fully convinced that slavery is sin and that it is the duty of God's children to turn much upside down, Shipherd communicated his confidence that the people of Oberlin are precisely those who should heed the call. "Who should be forward in these overturnings and inventions if not my dear people

30. Morris, *Hotbed of Abolitionism*, 27.
31. Morris, *Hotbed of Abolitionism*, 32.
32. Morris, *Hotbed of Abolitionism*, 32.
33. Shipherd, "Pastoral Letter," para 1.

at Oberlin?"[34] Shipherd's deep concern for the colony that once had only existed in his heart and mind was that external pressures would prevent them from doing what they know to be right. He described this exchange as choosing expedience over the conviction of duty. Shipherd described what he viewed to be much too prevalent in the church of his day—an acquiescence to fear that paralyzes the church from taking rightful action. Shipherd expressed his apprehension:

> My fears are excited by your recent expressions of unwillingness to have youth of color educated in our Institute. Those expressions were a grief to me, such as I have rarely suffered. Although I knew that with some of you the doctrine of expediency was against the immediate abolition of slavery, because slaves are not qualified for freedom, I supposed you thought it expedient and duty to elevate and educate them as fast as possible, that therefore you would concur in receiving those of promising talent and piety into our institution. So confident was I that this would be the prevailing sentiment of Oberlin in the colony and Institute that about a year ago I informed eastern inquirers that we received students according to character, irrespective of color; and, beloved, whatever the expediency or prejudice of some may say, does not duty require this? Most certainly.[35]

After expressing his grave concern that Oberlin was simply not the colony he had hoped it to be, Shipherd, in true expository fashion, offered twenty reasons why the Institute at Oberlin College must be the first in America to open wide their doors to students of color.

1. They are needed as ministers, missionaries, and teachers for the land of their fathers, and for their untaught, injured, perishing brethren of our country.
2. Their education seems highly essential if not indispensable to the emancipation and salvation of their colored brethren.

---

34. Shipherd, "Pastoral Letter," para 2.
35. Shipherd, "Pastoral Letter," para 4.

3. They will be elevated much more rapidly if taught with Whites, hitherto far more favored, than if educated separately.
4. The extremity of their wrongs at the White man's hand requires that the best possible means be employed, and without delay, for their education.
5. They can nowhere enjoy needed education unless admitted to our institution, or others established for Whites.
6. God made them of one blood with us; they are our fellows.
7. They are our neighbors, and whatsoever we would they should do unto us, we must do unto them, or become guilty before God. Suppose, beloved, your color were to become Black, what would you claim, in this respect, to be your due as a neighbor?
8. Those we propose to receive are the "little ones" of Christ. We must "take heed how we offend one of these 'little ones.'"
9. The objection to associating with them for the purpose of thus doing them good is like the objection of the Pharisees against our Saviour's eating with publicans and sinners.
10. Intermarriage with the Whites is not asked, and need not be feared.
11. None of you will be compelled to receive them into your families, unless, like Christ, the love of your neighbor compel you to.
12. Those who desire to receive and educate them have the same right to do it that Christ had to eat with publicans and sinners.
13. Colored youth have been educated at other institutions for Whites.
14. They will doubtless be received to all such institutions by and by, and why should beloved Oberlin College wait to do justice and show mercy till all others have clone it? Why hesitate to lead in the cause of humanity and of God?
15. Colored youth cannot be rejected through fear that God will be dishonored if they are received.
16. However it may be with you, brethren, I know that it was only the pride of my wicked heart that caused me to reject them while I did.

17. If we refuse to deliver our brother now drawn unto death, I cannot hope that God will smile upon us.
18. The men and money which would make our institution most useful cannot be obtained if we reject our colored brother. Eight professorships and ten thousand dollars are subscribed upon condition that Rev. C. G. Finney become Professor of Theology in our Institute, and he will not unless the youth of color are received. Nor will President Mahan nor Professor Morgan serve unless this condition is complied with. And they all are the men we need, irrespective of their anti-slavery sentiments.
19. If you suffer expediency or prejudice to pervert justice in this case you will in another.
20. Such is my conviction of duty in this case that I cannot labor for the enlargement of the Oberlin Collegiate Institute, if our brethren in Jesus Christ must be rejected because they differ from us in color.[36]

Shipherd pled with his flock at Oberlin to lead in the cause of humanity and of God. It seemed as if Shipherd was fully aware of this historical moment in the country and saw the need for convicted action on the part of those who claimed to follow Jesus. Shipherd also clearly delineated the costly price of inaction; he simply could not continue to labor for the cause of Oberlin if brothers and sisters in Christ were not welcomed because of the color of their skin. The ramifications of such a perversion of justice, in the view of Shipherd, was one that would have long-term effects on the establishment at Oberlin.

Shipherd closed with a declaration of his love and commitment to the mission of Oberlin. Shipherd contended that it "would be hard for me to leave that institution which I planted in much fasting and prayer and tribulation . . . for which I prayed without ceasing, laboring night and day, and watering it with my sweat and tears."[37] Nonetheless, he resigned to a future without Oberlin College if his beloved were not up to confronting the evil of

---

36. Shipherd, "Pastoral Letter," paras 3–4.
37. Shipherd, "Pastoral Letter," para 5.

slavery—the pressing sin of their age. Shipherd advanced that he had come to the decision "that if the injured brother of color, and consequently Brothers Finney, Mahan, and Morgan . . . must be rejected, I must join them; because by so doing I can labor more effectively for a lost world and the glory of God."[38]

Shipherd finished his letter on a winter day in antebellum New York with a vision of a hopeful reunion in the spring.

> And if on my return in April next, God willing, you, beloved flock, should still concur in desiring me to be your pastor, and concur in doing good to our oppressed brethren of color, I shall bless God for the privilege of wearing out as your servant for Christ's sake. As ever your affectionate brother, John J. Shipherd.[39]

---

38. Shipherd, "Pastoral Letter," para 5.
39. Shipherd, "Pastoral Letter," para 5.

Chapter 7
CASTE HAS FOUND NO ASYLUM

RISING TENSIONS

Shepherd's written pleas arrived at Oberlin College in the midst of a heated debate on the wisdom of accepting all students regardless of race. "From the point of view of the Oberlin trustees and students, Oberlin College's future rested on the Institute's willingness to accept Black students."[1] Prior to the arrival of Shepherd's letter in January 1835, the current students had decided to take matters into their own hands by circulating a petition in which students could sign their name as for or against the admission of Black students to the Institute. The majority of students were against such a policy, as thirty-two of the students declared themselves against and twenty-six voted in approval. Some of the female students even declared that "if Black students were admitted of equal privileges, they would return to their homes 'if they had to wade Lake Erie to accomplish it.'"[2]

Due to these rising tensions and the growing concerns of the students and surrounding community, a notice went out to the Oberlin College trustees on December 29, 1834, that their

---

1. Lesick, *Lane Rebels*, 170.
2. Morris, *Hotbed of Abolitionism*, 27.

upcoming meeting to discuss Shipherd's resolution would be moved from the colony of Oberlin to nearby Elyria. On January 1, 1835, the Oberlin trustees met in Elyria and with little fanfare unanimously elected Asa Mahan as the new President of Oberlin Collegiate Institute along with approving the appointment of John Morgan as teaching faculty. These motions from Shipherd were easily decided. The motion to admit Black students, however, was tabled. The board was hesitant to take an action that was divergent from the policies of all other higher education institutions in the country and did not feel adequately prepared to receive students irrespective of color. Finney recalled the confusion that dominated any discussion of slavery at that time as a "spirit that prevailed very extensively when Oberlin College was first established. Misrepresentations and misapprehensions abounded on every side; and these misapprehensions extended into almost every corner of the United States."[3]

Despite the early setbacks, the close vote of the students' petition was emblematic of what comprised, in all actuality, a far more progressive community than any within the surrounding area. Although Ohio carried the designation of a free state, "those African Americans who did settle within Ohio's borders were to be made as uncomfortable as possible and to acutely feel their supposed degradation."[4] The city of Cincinnati, where the Lane Theological Seminary Rebels were active in abolitionist efforts, had a horrific history of racist mob violence. If there was any sympathy for the plight of slaves, it was most often framed in the need for colonization, not immediate emancipation.

Even though it was surrounded by hostility, Shipherd held sincere hopes that the newly formed colony at Oberlin would ultimately come through and, in doing so, serve as a beacon in the darkness. He was so convinced that this was the correct course of action for the college that he went ahead and agreed to hire Mahan as president, guaranteed the students' demands, agreed to hire Morgan, and sought financial support from the Tappans, all

---

3. Finney, *Autobiography*, 314.
4. Morris, *Hotbed of Abolitionism*, 28.

before consulting the trustees. Shipherd's mind was made up, and his course had been chartered. If the trustees at Oberlin College could not agree to the terms as described, Shipherd would painfully part ways.

As the trustees mulled over the complex decision before them, Shipherd passionately wrote them from New York. Meanwhile, the students who had been working from the abandoned tavern in Cumminsville now saw a path forward. They longed to reconvene with Mahan and Morgan in Oberlin. Their resolve had been tested and been found true; they were not going to move without the guarantee of admission for all students, primarily their dear friend James Bradley. With such a vision seemingly so close to coming to fruition, the Lane Theological Seminary Rebels "were first and most vocal in their insistence that Oberlin live up to its Christian charter and potential by establishing a color-blind admissions policy."[5] In his account, Bradley described the acceptance and love he felt from his fellow students at Lane Theological Seminary: "But in all respects I am treated just as kindly, and as much like a brother by the students, as if my skins as white, and my education as good as their own."[6] If Bradley truly felt like a brother to the rest of the Rebels, how could his brethren acquiesce to the notion of attending a school where he could not be admitted, simply because of the color of his skin?

Shipherd was losing patience. He was ready to move forward and gravely disappointed by the trustees' hesitation as outlined in his January letter from New York. Oberlin was "established as a gathered community, supposedly of like mind . . . Now a majority of the Institute's trustees had exposed their individual shortcomings on a principle that a significant minority felt was absolutely essential to the continuance of the Oberlin experiment."[7] Everything else was in place and ready to commence once the conditions were met. The Lane Rebels in Cumminsville were ready to relocate to Oberlin. Likewise, Mahan, Morgan, and even Finney

5. Morris, *Hotbed of Abolitionism*, 32.
6. Bradley, "Brief Account," 689.
7. Morris, *Hotbed of Abolitionism*, 32.

were prepared to join the mission. All of this would fall apart, however, if the board would not pass Shipherd's resolution. Fletcher summarized the potential repercussions of further hesitation: "Unless the Oberlin trustees decidedly revised their stand on the question of the admission of Negro students the whole structure must collapse."[8]

Shipherd was disheartened by the delay and confused by the convictions, or lack thereof, of his beloved community. Even his dear friend and fellow Oberlin dreamer Philo Stewart had proclaimed Shipherd to be mad. As things began to unravel, Shipherd fearfully saw a growing number of similarities to the events at Lane Theological Seminary. He was convinced that the same curse that came to Lane would come to Oberlin if they could not pass this resolution. "After all, even Lane Theological Seminary had admitted African Americans into its ranks, including former slave James Bradley, who was also ready to enroll in the Oberlin Institute if they would have him."[9] Bradley, who had endured much more difficult trials in his pursuit of higher education, stood ready to become the first Black student admitted to an American institution of higher education by way of official policy if the Oberlin College Board of Trustees would see fit.

A REVOLUTIONARY POLICY

A little over a month removed from tabling Shipherd's resolution, on February 9, 1835, the board reconvened at Shipherd's home in Oberlin. The trustees once again debated the appropriate action to be taken. Three of the members clearly sided with the abolitionist, Nathan P. Fletcher, in support. Another three sided with fellow Oberlin College founder, Philo Stewart, in dissent. Thus, the deciding vote to be cast was in the hands of the newly appointed President of the Board of Trustees, Reverend John Keep. "The subject so enlisted the feelings of the pious inhabitants of Oberlin that

8. Fletcher, *History of Oberlin*, 175.
9. Morris, *Hotbed of Abolitionism*, 27.

Caste Has Found No Asylum

earnest and persevering prayer was offered, especially by a band of godly women."[10] Even with the prayers of these godly women and extensive, laborious discussion, the trustees were at a standstill and could not come to a resolution on February 9. The decision was rendered that the board should sleep on it and they adjourned until the next morning.

Perhaps only a good night's sleep was all that it finally required. On February 10, 1835, almost exactly one year from the first night of the historic debates at Lane Theological Seminary, Father John Keep cast the deciding vote in favor of Shipherd's resolution. Oberlin's place in American history was established for centuries to come. Lewis Tappan posited, "Caste has found no asylum or toleration at Oberlin since that day."[11] The Oberlin College Board of Trustees official meeting minutes recorded the historic resolutions:

> Whereas there does exist in our country an excitement in respect to our colored population, and fears are entertained that on the one hand, they will be left unprovided for, as to the means of a proper education, and on the other that they will in unsuitable numbers be introduced into our Schools, and thus in effect forced into the Society of Whites, & the state of public opinion is such as to regain from the Board some definite expression on the subject, therefore
>
> Resolved that the education of the people of color is a matter of great interest and should be encouraged in every proper way and manner & sustained in this Institution.[12]

Further, the Oberlin College Board of Trustees determined that day to put the power of admissions decisions firmly in the hands of the faculty. As has been noted by many historians, including Oberlin historian Robert Fletcher, Oberlin College was not the first institution to admit African American students. However, this

---

10. Fletcher, *History of Oberlin*, 240.
11. Tappan, *Life of Arthur Tappan*, 240.
12. Oberlin Board of Trustees Select Minutes, para 1.

was the first establishment of any official course of action anywhere in American higher education that clearly declared an institution open for admission for all students regardless of race. In contrast to being permitted to take classes at Lane Theological Seminary, James Bradley came to Oberlin College as a fully admitted student with equal opportunity and rights to every other student therein.

The historic impact of this decision could not have been immediately felt when Bradley arrived, but shortly thereafter Oberlin became as a city upon a hill for forward-thinking students from all over the country. Conservative interests suppressed abolitionists throughout the country, making Oberlin "about the only college left for young radicals to attend."[13] "From its opening in 1833 to the 1835 academic year, the student population grew by nearly 700 percent."[14] There was simply no room at all for the droves of students drawn to Oberlin, and yet they just continued to come and find a way just to partake in the revolutionary spirit alive and well in Oberlin, Ohio. "A capable and pious group of people had joined together in the West to become, as one Oberlin College trustee boasted, 'the decided opponent of slavery.'"[15]

The resolutions officially signed and all conditions clearly met, the Lane Rebels began to pack up their temporary home at Cumminsville, and many made the trek north to join Asa Mahan in Oberlin. Mahan arrived in May, and Charles Finney and John Morgan would join them at the beginning of the summer. Among the first of the Lane Rebels to arrive to enroll at Oberlin College was none other than James Bradley, who would become the first African American student under the newly established policy. With Bradley was William T. Allan, the one designated as president of the anti-slavery society and the first student targeted for dismissal by the Lane Board of Trustees. Joining them were John Alvord, Courtland Avery, and Enoch Bartlett, who would later serve as President of Olivet College. Lorenzo Butts was there too with Uriah Chamberlain, George Clark, and Charles Crocker.

13. Fletcher, *History of Oberlin*, 184.
14. Morris, *Hotbed of Abolitionism*, 38.
15. Morris, *Hotbed of Abolitionism*, 39.

Also among them were Amos Dresser, Benjamin Foltz, and Hiram Foote, who would later serve as a trustee for Rockford Female Seminary. In addition, there was David Ingraham, Deodat Jeffers, and Theodore Keep, the son of Father John Keep, who cast the deciding vote in favor of the resolution.

Huntington Lyman, Alexander McKellar, Israel Mattison, Lucius Parker, and Joseph Payne also enrolled. Also joining the group was the nephew of Arthur and Lewis Tappan, John Tappan Pierce, who would later be expelled from the state of Missouri for his anti-slavery efforts. Also among the rebels were Samuel Porter, C. Stewart Renshaw, Munson Robinson, Elisha Sherwood, William Smith, and James Steele. Sereno Streeter and James Thome would later become some of the most recognized among the rebels for their reflections on the formative experience of leaving Lane Theological Seminary and arriving at Oberlin College in Lorain County, Ohio.

Moreover, Samuel Thompson was a part of the group, along with George Whipple and Hiram Wilson, who would later work alongside fourteen other Oberlin College graduates to establish the British-American Institute of Science and Industry, a labor institute for Blacks, Whites, and Native Americans. Theodore Weld stayed with the group but never officially enrolled at Oberlin College, as he traveled the country spreading his abolitionist fervor. Lesick noted that historians recognize Allan, Alvord, Streeter, Thome, and Weld, along with Augustus Wattles, as those who carried the torch of abolition in the state of Ohio.

Historian Stephen Michael Tomkins wrote of a group of social reformers in London at the beginning of the nineteenth century, later to be known as the Clapham Sect. The chief accomplishment that this group is associated with is the Slavery Abolition Act of 1833. Tomkins wrote of this group of friends, "The ethos of Clapham became the spirit of the age."[16] Upon reflection on the lives and impact of these seminarian rebels, it may be said that their work rivaled that of their British counterparts at a time when the world was waking up to the moral depravity of slavery.

16. Tomkins, *Clapham Sect*, 248.

The ethos of the Lane Rebels became the spirit of the age in the antebellum West and blazed a trail upon which many would follow their example. "By the fall of 1835 Oberlin had quickly become a major center of anti-slavery activity in the West."[17] Finney's autobiography described these times at Oberlin College as times of divine influence. As he recalled these days at Oberlin he described the establishment of the town, which served as a key point for the Underground Railroad in the liberation of slaves. All of this resulted in what Finney declared a "state of universal confidence and good feeling between Oberlin and the surrounding regions."[18]

Shortly after the Lane Rebels arrival, an anti-slavery society was formed in Oberlin, this time, however, with the full support of the school's administration. The constitution of the Oberlin College Anti-Slavery Society founded in June of 1835 reads as a manifesto for the entire colony. Recorded in the Anti-Slavery Society's constitution are clearly delineated object, reason, and principle statements along with a determined mode of operation. The Anti-Slavery Society declared the mission as "the immediate emancipation of the whole colored race within the Unites States."[19] In addition, the objective of the Anti-Slavery Society is described as an effort toward "the emancipation of the slave from the oppression of the master, the emancipation of the free colored man from the oppression of public sentiment, and the elevation of both to an intellectual, moral, and political equality with Whites."[20]

The Anti-Slavery Society offered a theological condemnation of slavery:

> He is constituted by God a moral agent, the keeper of his own happiness, the executive of his own powers, the accountable arbiter of his own choice; personal ownership his birthright, unforfeited and invaluable; liberty, and the pursuit of happiness his chartered rights, inherited from his maker and guaranteed by all the laws of his being.

17. Morris, *Hotbed of Abolitionism*, 42.
18. Finney, *Autobiography*, 320.
19. Anti-Slavery Society, "Constitution," para 1.
20. Anti-Slavery Society, "Constitution," para 2.

> Slavery robs him of himself, body and soul; and though he is immortal, created in God's image, the purchase of a Saviour's blood, visited by the Holy Ghost, and united to a citizenship with angels and to fellowship with God, it drags him to the shambles and sells him like a beast, goads him to incessant and unrequited toil, withholds from him legal protection in all his personal rights and social relations, and abandons to caprice, cupidity, passion, and lust all that is dear in human well-being. It crushes the upward tendencies of the intellect, makes the acquisition of knowledge a crime, and consigns the mind to famine.[21]

The Oberlin College Anti-Slavery Society composed a constitution which described a strategy that involved "approaching the minds of slave holders with the truth, in the spirit of the Gospel."[22]

> Finally impelled by these considerations, and looking to God for wisdom, strength, and success, we solemnly pledge ourselves to each other, to seek through evil report and good report the immediate emancipation of the whole colored race. The emancipation of the slave from the oppression of the master, the emancipation of the free colored man from the oppression of public sentiment and the elevation of both to an intellectual, moral, and political equality with the Whites.[23]

Just days following the establishment of the society, Finney, Mahan, and Morgan were officially inaugurated on July 1, a day when a new age began in Oberlin. The curriculum was an exciting blend of biblical and theological tradition applied to the most pressing questions facing society. The discussion of social issues was seen as a distraction by the trustees at Lane Theological Seminary, but at Oberlin College, those topics could "easily be brought to bear on subjects as wide-ranging as political economy to moral philosophy."[24] The spirit of the age in Oberlin extended beyond

21. Anti-Slavery Society, "Constitution," para 3.
22. Anti-Slavery Society, "Constitution," para 21.
23. Anti-Slavery Society, "Constitution," para 35.
24. Morris, *Hotbed of Abolitionism*, 41.

the confines of the educational mission. "In Oberlin's early years, differentiating between the school and the community was nearly impossible, but largely unnecessary."[25]

JAMES BRADLEY AT OBERLIN

James Bradley arrived at Oberlin College in 1835, and by the end of the academic year, only two additional Black students had enrolled. During the antebellum period, Oberlin College would average a population of students of which only 2–5 percent were African American. "Though a small absolute number, more African American students were educated at Oberlin before 1860 than at all other American colleges combined, and the numbers increased almost every year."[26]

Oberlin College was a pioneer in the education of African American students joined by only a few others. One other institution, Oneida, sought to open their doors to Black students, but ultimately sent them to Oberlin. Oberlin College's African American students always believed that their own institution developed into one of the elite institutions of higher education in America. Among the students to study at Oberlin College during the antebellum era were the Langston brothers: Gideon, Charles, and John. Another family was the Edmonson sisters, Emily and Mary, who "had been rescued from the slave ship *Pearl* and supported at Oberlin College with funds provided by Harriet Beecher Stowe."[27] Slave rescue was a regular part of the Oberlin experience.

In seeking to summarize the historical impact of the college, Fletcher noted that "Oberlin College and Oberlin Collegeites were always ready to give aid to those Negroes who took their fate in their own hands. From the middle thirties to the Civil War, fugitives were constantly passing through Oberlin on the 'Underground

---

25. Morris, *Hotbed of Abolitionism*, 41.
26. Morris, *Hotbed of Abolitionism*, 67.
27. Morris, *Hotbed of Abolitionism*, 68.

Railway.'"[28] Oberlin College quickly became known as a hotbed of abolitionism where the ideas of immediate emancipation were expressed and safe harbor and liberation were provided to any slave. The antebellum era was a time of revolution at Oberlin College. "No one will ever know how many fugitives went north by way of Oberlin. One thing, however, is certain: all who came were hospitably received and cared for."[29]

The integration at Oberlin College was like few other places in antebellum America. "The 1850 census shows twenty-nine African Americans, many of them students, living in eighteen White households."[30] Oberlin College was also one of the first institutions where an African American female served as an instructor; Fanny Jackson Cooper taught in 1864 and 1865. "In a world that hated African Americans for the color of their skin, there did exist an exceptional community where Blacks and Whites could actually trust one another, love one another, and embolden each other toward greatness."[31]

While George Vashon would be the first Black student to earn an Oberlin College degree and Sarah Watson would be the first Black woman to enroll in 1842, it was James Bradley, against all odds, who was the first to arrive in the summer of 1835. In his memoir, former Oberlin College President James Harris Fairchild recounted the story of Bradley's arrival:

> A single colored student, James Bradley, once a slave, had come from Cincinnati, following the students from Lane Theological Seminary, with whom he had become acquainted. All the resistance to the reception of colored students, which had been exhibited less than a year before, had disappeared. All seemed to have forgotten that they could have cherished such feelings, and the colored brother was made perfectly at home.[32]

28. Fletcher, *History of Oberlin*, 395.
29. Fletcher, *History of Oberlin*, 396–97.
30. Morris, *Hotbed of Abolitionism*, 69.
31. Morris, *Hotbed of Abolitionism*, 72.
32. Fairchild, *Oberlin College*, 74.

The Light of Knowledge

Little is known of Bradley's time as a student. The Oberlin College archives show record of his enrollment at nearby satellite Sheffield Labor Institute. In a letter from James R. Wright to Elizur Wright Jr. written on April 4 1836, Wright recorded, "James Bradley is here; he will probably remain here for some time. In speaking of his journey here, he said that 'prejudice was so thick in some places that he could stir it with a stick.'"[33]

Bradley evidently stayed active in work of abolitionism in Ohio for many years. He was referenced in the *National Slavery Standard* on November 12, 1840:

> James Bradley, an emancipated slave, formerly of Lane Theological Seminary, speaking of the heaven-born and irrepressible longings of the slaves for freedom, gave utterance to his own feelings thus: Even liberty is bitter to me while my brethren remain in bondage.[34]

The archives at Oberlin also contain a copy of a written correspondence between James Bradley and Frederick Douglass sent from Ashland, Ohio, which shows Bradley's deep involvement in abolition as late as May 1848. Bradley wrote,

> Mr. Douglass—Dear Sir: I sit down to write you a few lines on behalf of my colored friends that were sold a few days ago from Washington to Georgetown. It makes my blood boil in my veins but I hope the Lord is with them, for they have been swindled out of their rights and robbed.
>
> I hope that every colored man in this state will improve his talents as I am trying to do myself, so that they may be able to advance the cause of millions in the South.[35]

Bradley recalled his arrival at Lane Theological Seminary in the brief account of his life that was published in the *Oasis*:

---

33. Wright, Letter, para 1.
34. National Slavery Standard, "James Bradley Quote."
35. Bradley, Letter, para 1.

As soon as I was free, I started for a free state. When I arrived in Cincinnati, I heard of Lane Theological Seminary, about two miles out of the city. I had for years been praying to God that my dark mind might see the light of knowledge. I asked for admission to the Seminary. They pitied me, and granted my request, though I knew nothing of the studies which were required for admission. I am so ignorant, that I suppose it will take me two years to get up with the lowest class in the institution. But in all respects I am treated just as kindly, and as much like a brother by the students, as if my skins as white, and my education as good as their own. Thanks to the Lord, prejudice against color does not exist in Lane Theological Seminary. If my life is spared, I shall probably spend several years here, and prepare to preach the gospel.[36]

Long after Bradley's death, a young Earl Billings played the role of James Bradley in a play that was written about Bradley and the Lane Theological Seminary Rebels arrival at Oberlin College. The play was produced near Cleveland in the 1960s and depicted Bradley's improbable journey—from his mother's arms in West Africa, to a slave ship on the Atlantic, to slavery in the South, to freedom in Ohio.

---

36. Bradley, "Brief Account," 688–89.

Epilogue

The Light of Knowledge

JAMES BRADLEY'S STORY IS one of fortitude and remarkable courage. Forced into slavery before his life could even truly begin, the devastating oppression Bradley experienced in the most troublesome moments of his life illuminates his valor. This valor was on grand display at the debates at Lane Theological Seminary, at his enrollment as the first African American student at Oberlin College, and, of course, in his resolute abolitionist determination for the remainder of his life. In 1835, the year that Bradley embodied the revolutionary policy at Oberlin College, he recalled his path to this revered colony. As Bradley reflected on all that was being done across antebellum America to liberate the oppressed, he penned these words:

> I will say but a few words more. My heart overflows when I hear what is doing for the poor broken-hearted slave, and free men of color. God will help those who take part with the oppressed. Yes, blessed be his holy name! He will surely do it.[1]

James Bradley arrived on the campus of Lane Theological Seminary determined to pursue an education. Throughout his life,

---

1. Bradley, "Brief Account," 690.

Epilogue

acquiring the light of knowledge was a dream he carried in his heart—through the painful and sudden separation from family as a child, multiple near-death experiences, and countless sleepless nights of labor. Bradley could have never known upon his arrival at Lane Theological Seminary that his experiences as a slave would help turn the tide of historic debates at the theological seminary founded at Walnut Hills. He could have never known that he would be the first African American student enrolled by way of an official institutional policy in American higher education. Bradley's insatiable desire for knowledge was rivaled only by the desire on display through the action of his Lane brethren, the purported seminarian rebels, which resisted the administration's attempt to silence their dialogue—dialogue that inspired love-informed action over the course of many lifetimes.

An ambition that first inspired this study was that the phenomena of student protest might be better understood using the historical events at Lane Theological Seminary and Oberlin College in 1834–35 as a case study. More specifically, that this historical case study could point toward the forms of protest or activism that engender enduring change, both at the institutions where they transpire and in society at large. In response to this stated ambition, the aftermath at both Lane Theological Seminary and Oberlin College offer a compelling tale of two cities.

LANE THEOLOGICAL SEMINARY

In the heat of the anti-slavery discussion, academic freedom was an endangered species on college campuses. In light of this, the conditions at Lane Theological Seminary in 1834 were conducive to a perfect storm. "It is not surprising the great test should have come at Lane Theological Seminary, for there was gathered an unusually mature and serious-minded group of students, led by a genius and inspired by the greatest preacher of the day."[2] Particularly influential among those students was Theodore Weld.

2. Fletcher, *History of Oberlin*, 150.

Influenced by the abolitionist movement across the Atlantic, Weld came to Lane Theological Seminary as a student to win the hearts and minds of the student body for the abolitionist cause.

Formally affiliated with the Presbyterian Church of the United States of America, Lane Theological Seminary opened its doors in 1830. The founding mission of Lane Theological Seminary was to prepare students for full-time service in ministry. Reverend Lyman Beecher served as the President of Lane Theological Seminary from 1832 to 1850. Reverend Beecher presided over the seminary throughout the time of the debates on the issue of slavery that transpired over the course of eighteen nights in February of 1834.

The seminary was still very young at the time of the debates, and the departure of the students who left Lane in the aftermath would have a lasting impact on sustaining the mission of the seminary in the Cincinnati area. Many of the students who left Lane Theological Seminary enrolled at Oberlin Collegiate Institute in northern Ohio, providing much-needed strength to the institution there. "By the end of the year, ninety-five of the 103 students previously enrolled at Lane Theological Seminary had left or not returned."[3]

Lane continued in its educational offerings into the twentieth century, but the institution would never recover from the Rebels' exodus in 1834. Lewis Tappan described President Beecher's acquiescence to the arbitrary rule of the trustees as a failure in leadership. "Born to be a leader, under some circumstances, this eminent man failed at this time in an essential attribute of leadership of moral and religious enterprises."[4] The Lane Rebels longed for an institution that would stand upon the foundation of free discussion as a means for learning. As they departed, the rebels prophesied the seminary's impending demise in their Statement of Reasons: *If institutions cannot stand upon this broad footing, let them fall.*

Lane Theological Seminary, founded with great hope, would never be the same; low enrollment lingered following the debates.

---

3. Lesick, *Lane Rebels*, 131.
4. Tappan, *Life of Arthur Tappan*, 233.

EPILOGUE

Eventually, Lane Theological Seminary merged streams with McCormick Theological Seminary in Chicago. The seminary's presence in Cincinnati diminished and "in the years that followed, evidence of the campus slowly began to disappear. Old buildings were torn down to make way for residential construction. The last remnant of the old seminary was demolished in 1956."[5] Documents from the institution's history in Cincinnati have been moved to Philadelphia to be preserved at the Presbyterian Historical Society.

OBERLIN COLLEGE

In his well-renowned volume on the history of higher education in America, historian John Thelin recognized Oberlin College as eminent in its commitment to offering educational opportunity to all. Thelin posited, "Oberlin Collegiate Institute would gain fame for its double commitment to coeducation according both to gender and race."[6] Such efforts toward equality have distinguished Oberlin College from its peers in the history of higher education. In her acclaimed text *In the Company of Educated Women*, Barbara Miller Solomon contextualized the educational environment at Oberlin College: "Here men and women, White and Black, were to be educated together to carry out God's cause on earth."[7]

Oberlin College stands as a testimony that the impact of a city or town is not merely determined by the size of the buildings or the geographic and industrial resources it provides, but rather by the human resources therein. "Oberlin College—the town, the college, the idea—has been remembered, if not fully understood, as one of the most powerful symbols of the American abolitionist movement."[8] This small town of just over eight thousand people in north-central Ohio—thirty-four miles southeast of

---

5. Ohio History Central, "Lane Theological Seminary."
6. Thelin, *History of Higher Education*, 55.
7. Solomon, *In the Company*, 21.
8. Morris, *Hotbed of Abolitionism*, 8.

The Light of Knowledge

Cleveland—and the college within would play a vital role in the eradication of slavery in America.

In tracing the history of the abolition of slavery in America, many important names and places ought to be remembered. The small town and college of Oberlin, Ohio, should be mentioned in the same company as many of its larger peers. "Oberlin was, beyond question, one of the most important communities in the abolitionist movement. In its symbolic and practical importance, it rivaled larger and more well-known eastern reform centers."[9] The size and scope of these abolitionist actions were embodied by men and women whose character and conviction abundantly overshadowed the size and scope of the town limits of this small Midwestern community.

Lane Theological Seminary and Oberlin Collegiate Institute were both founded during the antebellum era, when the question of slavery and how an institution responded to it captured the spirit of the age. Through extensive dialogue, reflection, and action, the students at Lane Theological Seminary experienced an education that led to liberating action. When the administration sought to silence the students, they felt they had no other option but to walk away from an institution they dearly loved—their minds made up, their hearts clear, the students displayed advanced critical thinking and steel in their spine. The protest of the Lane Rebels was one of theological conviction. In their zeal to follow in the steps of Christ, the students resolved to demonstrate his love to all, regardless of the color of skin.

Lane Theological Seminary would never be the same. The equal can be said of Oberlin College. The enduring change at Oberlin, however, is a very different tale. David Pilgrim, curator at the Jim Crow Museum, put the landmark decision of 1835 into perspective:

> By 1900, Oberlin College had produced one-third of all African American college graduates in the United States, including many who attained national prominence and historical significance such as Blanche Kelso Bruce, an

9. Morris, *Hotbed of Abolitionism*, 2.

Epilogue

ex-slave, the first Black American to serve a six-year term in the United States Senate; Moses Fleetwood Walker, the first Black player in professional baseball; Sarah Woodson Early, the first African American female college faculty person; and John Mercer Langston, Ohio's first Black lawyer. At the start of the Civil War, Oberlin enrolled more Black students than any other American institution of higher education.[10]

Oberlin Historian, J. Brent Morris commented, "The Oberlin community's utopianism, like that of its Pilgrim forbearers, was that of an intentional community . . . created as a deliberate effort to realize a specific goal or set of goals, in this case, the salvation of the world."[11] Nearly two centuries later, Oberlin College has over forty thousand alumni who followed those first students' example along the streets of this small town in Lorain County. Today, Oberlin College has a 440-acre campus and enrolls nearly three thousand students, of which the majority are women and 20 percent are students of color.

In 1858, a group of Oberlin and Wellington residents rescued a fugitive slave, John Price, from US Marshals, and took him to Canada. The case drew national coverage. Years later, the Oberlin-Wellington Rescue became known as "the incident that set the American Civil War in motion."[12] Among those involved in the Oberlin-Wellington Rescue, it has been speculated that none other than James Bradley played a critical role. The letter of student protest of 2016 described at the beginning of the book was the latest along a storied lineage of student activism that has enriched the educational environment at Oberlin College for nearly two hundred years. The changes at Lane Theological Seminary and Oberlin College are emblematic of the enduring change—for better and for worse—that thoughtful action by means of student protest can prompt at an institution for generations to come.

10. Pilgrim, "First College to Admit Blacks."
11. Morris, *Hotbed of Abolitionism*, 63.
12. Oberlin College, "Oberlin College History."

The Light of Knowledge

STUDENT PROTEST AND HIGHER EDUCATION

The historical events depicted in this book ought to prompt reflection for those who endeavor to lead at the modern university. Institutions should encourage the development of a pedagogy that resists the temptation to simply tell students what to think and join them in the thinking process, seeking dialogue with students, teaching them how to think. The students at Lane Theological Seminary simply could not comprehend the argument that was being made by their trustees. How, they questioned, is the discussion of the most pressing issue of the age considered a distraction to the course of study? It was for this very reason that the students selected a theological course that could inform their thinking and actions in response to society's most pressing concerns. To abandon discussion on slavery and restrict learning to the traditional form of theological training seemed treasonous to the students.

In similar fashion, the development of curriculum and the pedagogy modern educators employ should offer students many opportunities to apply what they are learning to the most pressing issues facing their world. The application of knowledge to such concerns is emblematic of the forms of high-impact deep learning the university exists to inculcate: "Education either functions as an instrument which is used to facilitate integration of the younger generation into the logic of the present system and bring about conformity or it becomes the practice of freedom, the means by which men and women deal critically and creatively with reality and discover how to participate in the transformation of their world."[13]

RECOMMENDATIONS FOR PRACTICE

The current state of higher education and the ubiquitous nature of student protest within provides educators opportunity for best practices to be implemented. Campus leaders, faculty, and students can create the conditions for such action to be seen not as

13. Freire, *Pedagogy of the Oppressed*, 34.

a disruption with destructive ends but rather a potentially rich developmental opportunity to demonstrate the power of dialogue. When any form of a protest transpires on a campus, it ought to serve as a pause for educational leadership to seek to understand the pain from which the protest is sourced. Ascertaining the pain of others is only possible through an earnest attempt to listen. As a result, campus leadership should seek to offer opportunities for dialogue with students to understand their experience. Such dialogue can be established through open forums designed around specific issues facing a campus or general talkback sessions designed to give students a voice.

While the onus is on academic leadership to establish a culture of dialogue, students who seek to bring concerns to light through the channel of protest would do well to follow the Lane Rebels' path of free discussion, reflection on duty, and determined action, which can serve to ground their decisions in protest and establish a foundation upon which enduring change can be built. The 2016 protest at Oberlin College described in the opening paragraphs of this study is a demonstration of a lack of dialogue. Upon reflection on the protest of the Lane Rebels, the establishment of dialogue ought to be considered as step one in the process of bringing about lasting change at an institution.

CONCLUSION

This is James Bradley's story. While there are many other aspects to the research and numerous applications to be made to understanding protest, pedagogy, and the essential nature of free discussion in higher education, this is a story to be told from the bottom up. It is a story that begins with a child ripped from his family and ends with a courageous liberator pleading the case of his brethren to Frederick Douglass. When Bradley arrived at Lane Theological Seminary, he found that he was "treated just as kindly, and as much like a brother by the students, as if my skin were as white, and my education as good as their own."[14] Bradley arrived at Lane Theological Seminary at a historical moment in antebellum America, and he would play a remarkable role in moving a nation forward through his enrollment at Oberlin.

Bradley's enrollment at Oberlin was the beginning of a momentous era there. Oberlin College became nationally known as the institution that "welcomed the outcasts with open arms."[15] Antebellum American higher education was largely being built on the backs of slaves, but in Lorain County, Ohio, John Shipherd dreamed of something much different. Oberlin College became "a beacon for the nation's most progressive students, and together with a thoroughly abolitionist faculty and community, they set about the mission of ridding America of its greatest and most pressing sin—slavery."[16]

Years later, Theodore Weld would look fondly upon those revolutionary days with his fellow seminarian rebels. Weld would occasionally write his friends and sought out any pictures and memories from their shared time at the seminary. "His old friends were understandably nostalgic about the events which had occurred at Walnut Hills so many years before."[17] The time spent together at Lane Theological Seminary and the events that transpired there were formative for the rest of their lives. Jennings's research described the long-term impact of student movements on the remainder of their lives and found that their participation in protest had enduring effects. The rebellion at Lane Theological Seminary chartered a course for the students that led to a lifetime involvement in the work for the abolition of slavery by way of immediate emancipation. Of the fifty-four rebels of which something is known, "forty-two engaged in anti-slavery activities after 1834. From the time of the Lane Theological Seminary rebellion to the end of the Civil War, the Lane Theological Seminary Rebels

14. Bradley, "Brief Account," 689.
15. Morris, *Hotbed of Abolitionism*, 3.
16. Morris, *Hotbed of Abolitionism*, 3.
17. Lesick, *Lane Rebels*, 167.

Epilogue

took part in, and sometimes led, numerous different anti-slavery endeavors."[18]

The motivating force for the rebels was rooted in their theological conviction. The term "evangelical" certainly engenders a far more complex conversation today than it once did; however, the evangelical faith of James Bradley and the Lane Theological Seminary Rebels serves as "a microcosm of evangelical America in its attempt to end the complex and frustrating problem of slavery, and to secure human rights in an unrighteous world."[19]

Huntington Lyman returned to Oberlin College fifty years from the time of the Rebels' first arrival as students. In retrospect, Lyman was no less certain of the actions he and his fellow students had taken.

> The winds of fifty winters have blown upon us, and the sedative of half a century since the events of my narrative were current has ministered its influence. The ardor of youth has departed and the western verge of life looms in the near distance. Oblivion waits before our gate. Those who took the step, long ago, adhere to the decision then made. For myself, I cannot see how we could have done differently in consistency with public duty or self-respect.[20]

Lyman's friend and fellow rebel, Sereno Streeter, revisited Cincinnati and the grounds of Lane Theological Seminary years later and shared a description of what he found in a letter to Theodore Weld. Street pondered what had transpired there some forty years previous and hoped that even though many of the Rebels were no longer among the living, that the actions they had taken would abide long after they were gone. In an appendix to his biography, Charles Grandison Finney noted that a man by the name of Joshua Leavitt was tasked with writing a history of the anti-slavery movement. Finney wrote of Leavitt's task, "He will do as well as many unacquainted with the influence of Oberlin on the whole

18. Lesick, *Lane Rebels*, 167.
19. Lesick, *Lane Rebels*, 237.
20. Lyman, "Rebels," 68–89.

The Light of Knowledge

Northwest. The fact is that Oberlin College turned the scale in all of the Northwest. No man can tell the story right unless he knows this."[21]

Through remarkable endurance, thoughtful witness, and reflective action, James Bradley created a world in which it is easier to love. His is a story to be remembered and told wherever the task of liberation is found. As he concluded the account of his life, James Bradley maintained great hope as he imagined a better future; "men of every color meet at the feet of Jesus, speaking kind words, and looking upon each other in love—willing to live together on earth as they hope to live in heaven!"[22]

---

21. Finney, *Autobiography*, Appendix 8.
22. Bradley, "Brief Account," 690.

Bibliography

Anti-Slavery Society of Oberlin College. "Constitution of the Oberlin College Anti-Slavery Society." www2.oberlin.edu/external/EOG/Documents/OberlinAntiSlaveryCon.htm.
Asbury, Herbert. "The Abolition Riots of 1834." *The New Yorker*, November 5, 1932.
Blassingame, John W. *Slave Testimony: Two Centuries of Letters, Speeches, Interviews, and Autobiographies*. Baton Rouge: Louisiana State University Press, 1977.
Bradley, James. "Brief Account of the Emancipated Slave Written by Himself." In *Slave Testimony: Two Centuries of Letters, Speeches, Interviews, and Autobiographies*, edited by John W. Blassingame, 686–90. Baton Rouge: Louisiana State University Press, 1977.
———. Letter to Frederick Douglass, 1848. Files on Students and Faculty, 1836–40, James Bradley Folder. Oberlin College Archives, Oberlin College.
Butts, Lorenzo. Request for Dismission, 1834. Folder 286-1-30, The Students and the Slavery Question. Presbyterian Historical Society Archives, Presbyterian Historical Society.
Cincinnati Pandect, September 8, 1829. Folder 286-1-30, The Students and the Slavery Question. Presbyterian Historical Society Archives, Presbyterian Historical Society.
Dickey, Jack. "The Revolution on America's Campuses." *Time Magazine Online*, May 31, 2016. http://time.com/4347099/college-campus-protests/.
Fairchild, James H. *Oberlin College: The Colony and the College, 1833–83*, 1883. Files on Students and Faculty, 1836–40. Oberlin College Archives, Oberlin College.
Finney, Charles G. *Charles G. Finney. An Autobiography*. London: Hodder & Stoughton, 1876.
Fletcher, Robert S. *A History of Oberlin College from Its Foundation through the Civil War*. Oberlin, OH: Oberlin College Press, 1943.
Freire, Paulo. *Pedagogy of the Oppressed*. New York: Continuum, 2000.

Bibliography

Gavins, Raymond. "A Historical Overview of the Barriers Faced by Black American Males in Pursuit of Higher Education." In *Black American Males in Higher Education: Diminishing Proportions*, edited by H. T. Frierson, W. Pearson, & J. H. Wyche, 13–29. Bingley, UK: Emerald Group, 2009.

Higher Education Research Institute (HERI). "The American Freshman: National Norms Fall 2015." https://www.heri.ucla.edu/briefs/TheAmericanFreshman2015-Brief.pdf.

Jennings, M. Kent. "Generation Units and the Student Protest Movement in the United States: An Intra- and Intergenerational Analysis." *Political Psychology* 23.2 (2002) 303–24.

———. "Residues of a Movement: The Aging of the American Protest Generation." *The American Political Science Review* 8.2 (1987) 367–82.

Kiesewetter, John. "Civil Unrest Woven into City's History." The Cincinnati Enquirer. https://www.cincinnati.com/story/news/blogs/our-history/2018/06/08/civil-unrest-woven-into-citys-history/685960002/.

Krislov, Marvin. "Response to Student Demands." Oberlin College Campus News. https://www.oberlin.edu/news/response-student-demands.

Lane Theological Seminary Board of Trustees. Charter and Amendments, 1832. Folder 286-1-30, The Students and the Slavery Question. Presbyterian Historical Society Archives, Presbyterian Historical Society.

———. Meeting Minutes, October 6, 1834. Folder 286-1-30, The Students and the Slavery Question. Presbyterian Historical Society Archives, Presbyterian Historical Society.

———. Meeting of the Executive Committee, August 20, 1834. Folder 286-1-30, The Students and the Slavery Question. Presbyterian Historical Society Archives, Presbyterian Historical Society.

Lesick, Lawrence T. *The Lane Theological Seminary Rebels: Evangelicalism and Antislavery in Antebellum America*. Metuchen, NJ: Scarecrow, 1980.

Lyman, Huntington. "Lane Theological Seminary Rebels." In *Oberlin College Jubilee, 1833–83*, 60–69. Oberlin College: E. J. Goodrich, 1883.

McCormick, Richard P. *The Black Student Protest Movement at Rutgers*. Piscataway, NJ: Rutgers University Press, 1990.

McMillan, James H., and Sally Schumacher. *Research in Education: Evidence-Based Inquiry*. New York: Pearson Higher Education, 2014.

Morris, J. Brent. *Oberlin College, Hotbed of Abolitionism: College, Community, and the Fight for Freedom and Equality in Antebellum America*. Chapel Hill: University of North Carolina Press, 2014.

National Slavery Standard. "James Bradley Quote on Slavery," November 12, 1840. Files on Students and Faculty, 1836–40, James Bradley Folder. Oberlin College Archives, Oberlin College.

Oberlin College. "Student Letter of Protest." Scribd.com. https://www.scribd.com/document/293326897/Oberlin-College-Black-Student-Union-Institutional-Demands.

———. "Oberlin History." https://www.oberlin.edu/about-oberlin/oberlin-history.

Bibliography

Oberlin College Board of Trustees. Select Minutes of the Oberlin College Board of Trustees, 1835. Oberlin College Archives, Oberlin College. https://isis2.cc.oberlin.edu/external/EOG/LaneDebates/OCBoardMinutes1835%20.htm.

Ohio History Central. "Lane Theological Seminary." https://ohiohistorycentral.org/w/Lane_Theological_Seminary.

Orum, Anthony M. *Black Students in Protest: A Study of the Origins of the Black Student Movement.* Washington, DC: American Sociological Association, 1972.

Osofsky, Gilbert, Henry Bibb, William Wells Brown, and Solomon Northup. *Puttin' on Ole Massa: The Slave Narratives of Henry Bibb, William Wells Brown, and Solomon Northup.* American Perspectives Series. New York: Harper & Row. 1969.

Pilgrim, David. "First College to Admit Blacks—June 2010 Question." Ferris State University. https://www.ferris.edu/HTMLS/news/jimcrow/question/2010/june.htm.

Presbyterian Historical Society. "Lane Theological Seminary." Folder 286–1-30, The Students and the Slavery Question. Presbyterian Historical Society Archives, Presbyterian Historical Society.

Rael, Patrick. *Black Identity and Black Protest in the Antebellum North.* Chapel Hill: University of North Carolina Press, 2001.

Rudolph, Frederick. *The American College and University: A History.* Athens, GA: University of Georgia Press, 1990.

Shipherd, John Jay. "Pastoral Letter." Oberlin College Online Archives. https://www2.oberlin.edu/external/EOG/History268/shipherd.html.

Solomon, Barbara. M. *In the Company of Educated Women: A History of Women and Higher Education in America.* New Haven: Yale University Press, 1985.

Stanton, H. B. "Great Debate at Lane Seminary. Debate at the Lane Theological Seminary, Cincinnati: Speech of James A. Thome, of Kentucky, delivered at the annual meeting of the American Anti-Slavery Society, May 6, 1834." Boston: Garrison & Knapp, 1834. https://digital.history.pcusa.org/islandora/object/islandora:176446#page/1/mode/1up.

Stowe, Harriet Beecher. *Uncle Tom's Cabin; or, Life Among the Lowly.* Boston: John P. Jewett, 1952.

Students' Request for Dismission, 1834. Lane Theological Seminary Rebels. Folder 286-1-30, The Students and the Slavery Question. Presbyterian Historical Society Archives, Presbyterian Historical Society.

Students' Statement of Reasons. Statement of Reasons, 1834. Folder 286-1-30, The Students and the Slavery Question. Presbyterian Historical Society Archives, Presbyterian Historical Society.

Stripling, Jack. "Thrust into a National Debate on Race, Two Missouri Chiefs Resign." *The Chronicle of Higher Education*, November 10, 2015. http://chronicle.com/article/Thrust-into-a-National-Debate/234131.

Tappan, Lewis. *The Life of Arthur Tappan.* New York: Hurd & Houghton, 1871.

Bibliography

Thelin, John. R. *A History of American Higher Education*. Baltimore: Johns Hopkins University Press, 2011.

Tomkins, Stephen. *The Clapham Sect: How Wilberforce's Circle Transformed Britain*. Oxford: Lion, 2010.

Van Dyke, Nella. "Hotbeds of Activism: Locations of Student Protest." *Social Problems* 45.2 (1998) 205–20.

Weld, Theodore. *American Slavery as It Is: Testimony of a Thousand Witnesses*. New York: American Anti-Slavery Society, 1839.

———. Letter from Theodore Weld, 1835. Files on Students and Faculty, 1836–40, James Bradley Folder. Oberlin College Archives, Oberlin College.

———. Request for Dismission, 1834. Folder 286-1-30, The Students and the Slavery Question. Presbyterian Historical Society Archives, Presbyterian Historical Society.

Wilder, Craig Steven. *Ebony and Ivy: Race, Slavery, and the Troubled History of America's Universities*. New York: Bloomsbury, 2013.

Wright, James. Letter to Elizur Wright Jr., April 4, 1836. Files on Students and Faculty, 1836–40, James Bradley Folder. Oberlin College Archives, Oberlin College.

www.ingramcontent.com/pod-product-compliance
Lightning Source LLC
Chambersburg PA
CBHW072147160426
43197CB00012B/2287